UNFOLDING THE UNCONSCIOUS PSYCHE

Unfolding the Unconscious Psyche is a study of the creative arts and depth psychology, and the threads that run between the two. Edward Applebaum begins with works of art, in media including painting, music, literature and film, and pursues aspects of each to aid understanding of the unconscious psyche of the creator.

By combining a study of the artistic work with the insight of depth psychology, Applebaum opens a dialogue between studies of works of art and their creators and the individuals who form the audience for such works. Each discussion is dictated by the artwork itself and is viewed from a variety of perspectives. Throughout the book readers are encouraged to develop their own analytical technique: to follow the clues available, link threads together and analyse what they can see. The result demonstrates the value of dialogue in blending depth psychology with the arts, through examination of work by artists including Georgia O'Keeffe, Ingmar Bergman, Frida Kahlo, Gustav Mahler and Virginia Woolf. Applebaum also seeks to correct misconceptions about the arts that have filtered into the study and practice of depth psychology since the earliest writings of Freud and Jung.

This uniquely creative and insightful work will be absorbing reading for analytical and depth psychologists, students of analytical psychology, academics and scholars of the arts and anyone with an interest in the application of Jungian ideas.

Edward Applebaum is a composer whose music has been performed in the US and abroad. He has been awarded grants in composition, neurosciences and higher education. His Symphony No. 2 was awarded the Kennedy Center Friedheim Award. He has taught at universities in the US, Norway and Australia.

'Edward Applebaum succeeds virtuosically in transforming how we understand creativity in these close readings of how symbols are transformed between the unconscious and consciousness of representative artists. His book is therefore not only for those interested in analytic psychology but also for any layperson, artist, or academic.

Drawing on Jung's conviction that art is a major pathway by which the psyche finds balance and integration, Applebaum achieves a "total work of *understanding*" which synthesizes the creative arts and psychology. In seeking to "unfold" the psychic processes of representative artists, Applebaum also uncovers previous misunderstandings of the creative process itself. Each of Applebaum's case studies illuminates both a work of art and the psyche of the individual who created it. Specific artists discussed range from Gustav Mahler, F. Scott Fitzgerald, and Virginia Woolf to Georgia O'Keefe, Ingmar Bergman, and Frida Kahlo – and many others.

Applebaum's generosity is abundantly on display here. In a sense, he is giving back to those who have experienced his creativity as a musical composer, supporting those who listen and attend carefully – both to him and themselves.'

—David Brenner, University of Houston, USA.

'Out of Edward Applebaum's vast didactic and psychological experience comes a brilliant synthetic expression for artists, psychologists and those interested in creative process.

In this book he helps readers enter the creative experience of both the artist and the audience/recipient: the transcendent function in action. In other words, artists of all kinds are such because they can contact and express the gift in their unconscious which allows the audience to expand in a similar way.'

—Deanne Kreis Newman, Jungian Analyst, Santa Fe
New Mexico, USA.

UNFOLDING THE UNCONSCIOUS PSYCHE

Pathways to the Arts

Edward Applebaum

Routledge
Taylor & Francis Group
LONDON AND NEW YORK

First published 2016
by Routledge
27 Church Road, Hove, East Sussex BN3 2FA

and by Routledge
711 Third Avenue, New York, NY 10017

Routledge is an imprint of the Taylor & Francis Group, an informa business

British Library Cataloguing in Publication Data
A catalogue record for this book is available from the British Library

Library of Congress Cataloging in Publication Data
Applebaum, Edward.
Unfolding the unconscious psyche: pathways to the arts/Edward Applebaum.—
1 Edition.
pages cm
1. Subconsciousness. 2. Arts—Research. I. Title.
BF315.A6697 2016
154.2—dc23
2015006189

ISBN: 978-1-138-81931-3 (hbk)
ISBN: 978-1-138-81932-0 (pbk)
ISBN: 978-1-315-73983-0 (ebk)

Typeset in Bembo and Stone Sans
by Florence Production Ltd, Stoodleigh, Devon, UK

CONTENTS

FOREWORD

From the limited purview of ordinary consciousness, the problem with the unconscious is that it is *unconscious*, which is to say we can say nothing about what we cannot know. And as Ludwig Wittgenstein reminds us, 'Whereof we cannot speak, thereof we should remain silent.' Edward Applebaum productively undertakes, however, a most ambitious project: to talk about that which cannot be talked about.

When Freud, Breuer, Jung and other pioneers of modern depth psychology began, they frequently reached the end of their branches of learning and instrumentalities, and found it necessary to find new ways to track that which remained most puzzling, most elusive, namely, why were their patients having these debilitating symptoms when no neurological origins could be found? They painstakingly realized that what happens to us, through us and in spite of us might be tracked by way of symptomatology into the places of wounding, venues of displacement and, most of all, into symbolic expressions for that which could not be articulated by consciousness alone. They made the imaginative leap that brought self-understanding to a whole new level; namely, however 'crazy' it seems at the moment, what we do is 'logical', based on the premises operating within. Such premises are often infantile 'readings' of the world, fallacious assumptions, spurious causal events – but their manifestation in somatic, cognitive or behavioural life is a logical expression of those hidden sources.

When examining artistic productions of all kinds, Freud seemed compelled to see them as the by-products of the frustrated libidinal life of the artist; and often they may be. Jung included art as one of the many ways in which the psyche seeks to find wholeness, heal itself, by bringing unconscious contents to the surface so that they might be incorporated into an enlarged conscious conduct of life. For both, the arts were symbolically significant: either manifesting blocked libidinal drives seeking vicarious, symbolic relief, or as impulses of the psyche healing itself by incorporating its multiplicitous contents.

Each of us has noticed this phenomenon of something activated within which reaches the surface unexpectedly in a troubling dream, a song that imposes itself upon us, a recurrent image that brings up an affect unbidden by consciousness. For example, I have often examined why a particular lyric persists unbidden and I usually find that its content is giving expression to some issue that I may or may not be addressing consciously. When I was in training in Zürich decades ago I frequently visited the Kunsthaus, or city art gallery. No matter what corridor I went down, I always found myself standing before a battered Roman statue of the flaying of the satyr Marsyas. When, after I noticed this peculiar repetition, I did some research on the subject of this tormented stone, I found amazing parallels with my inner process at that moment. In other words, something in my psyche was activated by, and responding to, the psychic disturbance of an unknown sculptor millennia ago who invested stone with the stuff of spirit sufficient to move a later soul.

We have such experiences frequently: an image comes, persists and then disappears. A dream motif intrudes, and perseverates for several weeks. Each of these occasions is a moment when the two worlds – outer and inner – meet in noticeable ways. Most of the time they are meeting in ways unnoticed by the harried ego. Jung described such meetings as examples of the 'transcendent function', namely, the autonomous activity of the psyche to heal itself by bringing these disparate worlds together, to anneal the splits within us that bring so much suffering to us, and through us to others.

As a psychoanalyst, my daily work is to look for such apertures into the unconscious scattered amid the visible wake we leave in the world. We swim in these manifestations: patterns of behaviour, dream motifs, sudden flashes of affect-laden imagery, imaginative productions such as art, and the like. The psyche is never silent, never passive. It is always at work, not only maintaining the multiplicitous operations of the body that no ego could manage, and furthering the possible cooperation of the conscious and unconscious worlds. On those occasions when the two worlds meet, either healing or more pathology emerges.

Edward Applebaum comes to this study with a rich and varied background. He is a world-class composer of symphonies, a gifted instructor of music history and composition in some of our finest universities, a Mahler expert, and a long-time student of depth psychology. He brings this rich experience to bear in *Unfolding the Unconscious Psyche*, demonstrating that those arts also provide pathways into the depth dynamics, and dimensions, of our own souls.

*

Armed both with scholarship and his own imaginative gifts, Applebaum brings wit, insight and a genuine creative process to his subjects. For example, while Mahler suffers his wife's infidelity, he labours to complete his tenth symphony, a symbolic barrier (a step beyond the god Beethoven), which he believes may also presage his early death, as indeed it does. We know Freud and Mahler met briefly in an analytic session, Freud concluding that the composer's work was, only, a symptom of the composer's blocked sexual libido. Theoretically, had libido not been so blocked, there would be no symphony. Applebaum speculates on how a meeting with Jung might have transpired, a meeting in that the impulse to write music is most of all serving the *daimon* with which Mahler was both gifted and burdened, and a heroic effort to bring his own deeply separated soul into final harmony.

As another example of brilliant juxtaposition of these contiguous worlds we inhabit, Applebaum explores one of the finest novels of psychoanalysis ever written, F. Scott Fitzgerald's *Tender is the Night.* While the novel is a barely concealed *roman à clef,* psychiatrist Dick Diver tracks the progression of his beloved to where she is sadly unable to hold the tension of opposites and descends into a psychotic withdrawal. The normal unities of past, present and future collide in a psyche where the ego is no longer able to tell them apart. Just as Fitzgerald himself later descends into an alcohol-fuelled *catabasis*, so the ego seems pulled apart by the opposites. Reportedly, James Joyce once brought his distressed, schizophrenic daughter Lucia to Jung who said to the writer, 'Your daughter is drowning in that sea in which you learned to swim.' No one better expressed the power of the unconscious with its plethora of contents thrown up into the ego consciousness autonomously than Joyce, and no one ever maintained a greater dialogue with those spindrift images than the exile from Dublin. Both Joyce and Fitzgerald were self-styled exiles from their homelands, and both expressed their longing, their aspirations and their griefs in forms that healed because containing the opposites otherwise, daily, threatened to destroy or devour them.

Exploring artists as disparate as Ingmar Bergman, Beethoven, Kahlo, Rivera, Munch, Woolf, Durrell, the timeless zone of the *Märchen* known to us as 'the fairy tales', O'Keeffe, Ibsen, Strindberg and modern filmmakers, Applebaum demonstrates over and over the ineluctable force of something buried within the creator that is wishing expression through them. This parturient process comes, as any baby arrives, as a painful but profoundly powerful encounter with the divine forces that move us.

★

So often we ask of the world, 'What do you want from me?' What do parents want? What does the teacher want? What does the employer want? What does the partner want? What does the tribe want? These are reality-based questions and demand the development of a capable ego capacity to meet these demands as best one can. Such is the agenda of the first half of life. However, somewhere along the way, something else begins to stir within each of us. The more we have done what we are supposed to do, the more we have met the demands of the world – with more or less success – the more disturbing this insurgency from below. For some it will appear as a nagging dis-ease, a lack of satisfaction in what has been achieved. For others it will arise as an affective disturbance such as depression or an anxiety disorder. For others it will come as a jarring dream, or waking at 'the hour of the wolf' and feeling the desolation of an otherwise abundant life. It is in those moments that another question begins to emerge: *what does the soul want of me?* or *what wants to enter the world through me?*

Just as most of us expect that our 'success' in life will arise from meeting the world's expectations with as much accomplished energy as we can manage, or we ask more directly, 'what do I want from the world?' so this different question comes as an affront, a challenge, a threat even. Yet, the wisdom of the second half of life asks all of us, why, in addition to the puny but understandable agenda of ego consciousness, are we here? In service to what, really? To begin to ask oneself what wants to enter the world *through* me is to be called humbly before a mystery.

Applebaum appreciates fully the fact that the artist, like all of us in our different ways, is a vehicle for energies transcendent to the ego state. He knows that, as for most of us along life's anfractuous path, every artist is called to struggle, sacrifice comfort and control and, most of all, is summoned to service. In fact, one may say again that the chief summons of the second half of life is to be compelled to address the question*: not what does the world want of me, but what does the soul ask of me?* What is worthy of my service, whether it brings me recognition by others, or comfort, or happiness? In fact, most of the figures in history we most would admire suffered greatly, and left behind as their gift the tangible contributions of their soul's summons. So it is for the artist; so it is for the rest of us.

Whether triggered by pain, conflict, yearning, moments of sublimity, the end of art, Applebaum asserts, is to bring the unconscious world into the conscious, in the hope that the latter be enlarged, and the two worlds reside in some greater concord. In psychoanalytic terms, the meeting of these two worlds always collides in some sort of *image*, and the task of analysis is to track the image until we can discern what this meeting may mean to us, and even more, what it may be asking of us. When we recall that symbols are the means by which the inexpressible may be expressed, or at least presented to consciousness, then we realize that only the experience of, followed perhaps by the interpretation of, the symbol allows these two worlds to meet in non-pathologizing forms. We may not know the anatomy of any given effect, or how art does its work on us, but we are moved and changed by it, and brought into an enlarged space.

Years ago I had the privilege of knowing a very gifted painter, Nancy Witt of Ashland, Virginia. Nancy had her paintings in museums, corporate headquarters and in the hearts of so many of us. One night when we were talking about her work, she said that the review that meant most of all to her occurred when her work had been installed in a New Hampshire hotel for a conference on psychoanalytic themes. She overheard one of the workers, unlettered in the nuances of artistic techniques, and not an habitué of museums, call his colleagues over with excitement, saying to them, 'Come here, you have to see this. These are religious paintings.' Such a comment on her surrealistic oils was for her the highest possible accolade: she knew that that arrangement of colour and texture on canvas, arising from what unknown places in her soul, reached across the cultural gaps and touched the souls of others on this planet. When we can further enlarge consciousness through some sense of the meaning of any work, however idiocentric to us, consciousness becomes all the more capacious. It is that goal that Applebaum pursues in this study, and the gift that this book brings to the reader.

Historically, it was the task of the theologian and the mystic to track the movement of the invisible world through the cerements of the visible world. And it still is. As existential philosopher/*Daseinsanalyst* Karl Jaspers indicated, our modern task is 'to read the ciphers'; that is, to discern the clues of personal and cultural distress, to see the compensatory movements of symbolic expression, and to learn which values are missing, which are crying out for expression or embodiment in the world, and which are seeking the healing of person or tribe. Over the last two centuries, it has increasingly fallen to the student of the arts, and to the depth psychologists, to undertake the same project.

Our examinations of such transports and transformations of energy were perhaps best articulated a century ago by Jung in his 1912 *Symbols of Transformation.* This is the seminal work in which he broke from Freud, where he averred that the spontaneous act of symbol-making was less in reductive service to blocked instinctual drives than to the psyche's effort to heal itself and to further the dialectic between the visible and the invisible world. I can think of no higher praise for this book than to say that *Unfolding the Unconscious Psyche* follows Jung's impulse, and like Jung's work, adds so much to what we can know about that invisible world that courses through us, through history and through the souls of the artists.

James Hollis, PhD
Jungian analyst and author
Washington, DC

PREFACE

Otto Rank once referred to an important film he had seen as a 'romantic drama'.[1] The idea stemmed from a section in the book cited that introduces the basic concept of the relationships between psychoanalysis and the arts: using manifest conscious material to uncover the latent, the unconscious. The complexities inherent in utilizing psychoanalytical concepts to explore the arts – and vice versa – are beautifully described in a thought of one of the characters in Durrell's *Balthazar*, where he attempts to weave together the many events and characters who are continually reappearing.[2] The interweaving of the arts and the psyche are explored in the language we choose to use. We will encounter this in all of the media discussed.

Pathways into the arts illuminate our understanding of them – if only we allow them to develop a language that does not deviate from their reality. But we have difficulties in accepting the artist's reality and constantly attempt to (re)define it in language that is often meaningful to everyone except the person on whose art the discussion centres.

Example 1: In a recent interview, filmmaker Joe Wright in discussing his recent film *The Soloist*, as well as earlier films that he directed (*Atonement*, *Pride & Prejudice*), described how dyslexia informs his artistic process. 'It means you're forced to think about things in different ways and create different connections. I don't think in words so much. I think more in moments of film.' 'I think in moments of film in relationship between sound and image and how they come together in temporal moments.'[3] Wright was undiagnosed until relatively late in his life. He was considered lazy or stupid.

Example 2: Oliver Sachs on the mystery of creativity: 'Scientists can confirm that musically creative people continually have tunes in their heads, and they're incessantly playing with music themes. But I don't think that neuroscience can do more than confirm what talking to any composer would tell you.'[4]

The clearest presentation of this issue appears in a review of Frame's *Towards Another Summer*. New Zealand rehabilitation physician Sarah Abrahamson notes: 'From an early age, Janet (Frame) developed a strong interest in poetry, which was to become a lifelong interest. This appears to have been sufficiently intense to be considered an autistic "special interest".'[5] Poets and novelists, who persist in the pursuit of those 'interests' of theirs, may seize on that passage as evidence that a segment of the psychological community would want to pathologize genius.

Yes: I can imagine all of these examples. I've lived with them all my life.

As if we lived in a digital world where the brain now becomes a metaphor for the computer, science continually poaches on territory where it must redefine a world it does not know, and then quote itself as if it does.

*

All of the works of art that I will discuss are variations on a single theme. That theme is bringing the unconscious into consciousness through the creative arts. In their various genres, they form a journey of discovery. They dramatically extend the boundaries of their respective artefacts: words become music, vision becomes poetry, sounds become colours. Senses are redefined as we retrace the passages and symbolic transformations from the unconscious psyche to consciousness.

What are these transformations, and how do they occur?

References

1 Rank, O. *The Double*. Raleigh, NC: University of North Carolina Press, 1971, p. 3.
2 Durrell, L. *Balthazar*. New York: Dutton, 1958, p. 125.
3 Vigil, D. '*Soloist* director enjoys beating the odds'. *Houston Chronicle*, 23 March 2009, pp. E1, E8.
4 Sachs, O. 'Tunes in our heads'. *AARP Magazine*, June–February 2008, p. 24.
5 Gates, D. 'The visit'. *New York Times*, 17 May 2009, p. 7.

ACKNOWLEDGEMENTS

I would like to express my gratitude to those at Routledge who were so helpful in the process of bringing this book to life. In particular, Helen Hunt's Editorial Department and Kelly Derrick's consistently patient aid, Paris West's quick responses to my questions regarding marketing, and most of all, my Editor Susannah Frearson – mere words are impossible. Thank you all.

PART ONE

Music to create a universe

1

THEME: PART 1

The Haunting Melody

In many of our lives, there is a particular work of art that has had a profound and lasting effect upon us. In my case, it is a book about a symphony – Mahler's *Symphony No. 2* in Theodor Reik's *The Haunting Melody*. Over the years, I have read and reread Reik's work many times. It has greatly influenced the creation of this book.

The journey that is this book began with a phone call. A colleague of Freud's phoned Reik to inform him of the death of Karl Abraham; Abraham was an important member of Freud's group in Vienna. Freud had asked that Reik deliver a eulogy at a commemorative service for Abraham. Reik accepted.

To collect his thoughts, Reik took a walk in the cold wintry night. While walking, sounds of a particular piece of music invaded his consciousness – unbidden. The music was the concluding movement of Mahler's *Symphony No. 2*. It haunted Reik for several weeks, disappearing only when the eulogy was completed.

The story could have ended there. But the nature of Reik's training and analytic experience, both as analysand and analyst, compelled him to ask a simple question: Why this particular music?

To find the answer to this question, Reik engaged in a process of personal archaeology. He began with the part of the puzzle that seemed immediately manifest: the meaning of the music.

In *The Haunting Melody* and other writings on psychoanalysis and music, Reik mainly focused upon the dramatic and metaphoric aspects of the texts. In his essay 'The Three Women in a Man's Life' on the opera *The Tales of Hoffmann*, his concentration was upon the drama. In the essays preceding his exploration of Mahler in *The Haunting Melody*, his concentration was upon the texts.

This is how the process worked in his examination of the Mahler symphony. Several quotations from the text of the last movement of *No. 2* illustrate Mahler's concern with immortality:

You will rise again, my heart, in a moment,
And be borne up through struggle, to God.

Believe, my heart, you have lost nothing.
Everything you longed for is yours, yes, yours.
You have not lived and suffered in vain!

Yes, I am afraid, yes, I am afraid
That for resurrection we have long to wait.[1]

The subject of immortal life led Reik, through thought-association, to Goethe, who also believed in immortal life, and his meeting with the poet Heine . . . Goethe seemed to dislike Heine and Beethoven . . . Beethoven was born in Karlsbad, in Bohemia . . . Mahler was born in Kalischt, also in Bohemia . . .

In an analytic sense, three points had been introduced: (1) the criticism of the older for the younger, which becomes increasingly obvious; (2) the importance of the music of Beethoven, who thrust music into both the nineteenth and twentieth centuries by generating music that is organic – creating large works from a single idea; and (3) the subject of death. The haunting of the chorale from *No. 2* had something to do with the conquest of death and immortality:

I shall die so as to live . . .[2]

The emotional nature of the melody's emergence from Reik's unconscious, the haunting, served as a catalyst for Reik's explorations. He heard the music, but focused upon the text. That melody and text formed a symbiotic relationship in Reik's mind is understandable. Clearly, the music was in service to the text; however, music alone, without text, can elicit the same emotions – undifferentiated, as we shall see in Chapter 3 on Mahler and his third and ninth symphonies.

Reik's journey led him to Mahler's thoughts on creativity:

My need to express myself musically and symbolically starts where the dark emotions begin, at the door leading to the 'other world,' the world in which things are not any more separated by time and place.

While the first three movements tell the story [of the hero's death and burial] the last one is all inner experience.[3]

He learned of Mahler's obsession with death: Mahler's siblings and parents (who died while he was composing the first movement of *No. 2*, called a funeral march), and later his daughter. The death of Hans von Bülow, and Mahler's attendance at the funeral, was the reason Mahler heard the music that was to become the haunting episode for Reik; he continued his journey of discovery by next delving into Mahler's biography.

Mahler had reached a creative impasse; he was unable to complete his second symphony. While *Symphony No. 1* heralded the birth of the hero, the first movement of *No. 2* portrayed the hero's death. Mahler's struggles with the conclusion of this symphony were interrupted by a funeral for Hans von Bülow, the most important conductor of the time. As Mahler entered the church, the choir began singing a hymn with a text by the German poet Klopstock. Mahler had a sudden inspiration, the solution to his creative impasse – this poem/hymn became the concluding movement of his second symphony – the Resurrection. Immortality.

Von Bülow had played a significant role in furthering Mahler's conducting career. Upon his death, Mahler's career ascended, aided by his new position as conductor and music director of the Vienna Opera. Mahler thus benefited from the death of von Bülow.

Von Bülow was Mahler's senior. He supported Mahler's conducting career, but when Mahler played him the music to the first movement of *No. 2*, he hated it. Abraham was Reik's training analyst and, later, good friend. Karl Abraham thought very highly of Reik as a writer, and supported the contributions he would make in his writings. But he was against lay analysis. Abraham believed that psychoanalysts should be physicians; Reik was not a medical doctor, but a PhD.

The conditions facing Reik were strikingly similar to those under which Mahler found the solution to the ending of his second symphony. Both Reik and Mahler were supported by older colleagues. Both benefited from the death of these colleagues, and each was personally involved in these colleagues' rites of passage after their deaths. It was the conquest of the mentor by the disciple: Reik dreamt of elevation within Freud's inner circle, while Mahler saw the way being cleared for him to assume the position at the Vienna Opera. The emergence of both Reik and Mahler was aided by the death of a mentor. Reik questioned whether there were death wishes involved.

Neither the Abraham/Reik nor the von Bülow/Mahler relationships were in balance. There were existential tensions between them. And although the discovery of the linkage was a critical feature in Reik's fragmentary self-analysis, Mahler did not suffer from von Bülow's conditional admiration, whereas Reik did suffer from Abraham's. Mahler finished his symphony very quickly, while Reik took over thirty years to fully understand and write his book on the haunting melody.

Reik was suffering from the same sort of creative block as Mahler at the time Mahler heard the Klopstock hymn. The basic question remained: why music? And why this particular music? Having come so far, Reik was unable to complete his study of the melody's haunting. He still felt that the small incident had not yet been fully explained.

His thought (re)associations led him in this way: the melody which haunted him was somehow related to death . . . death was a subject that haunted Mahler all his life: his siblings, his parents, his daughter, himself, his own death . . . *Kindertotenlieder*, *Das Lied von der Erde*, *Symphony No. 9*.

From an additional perspective, the complexity of Mahler's use of the choir in *No. 2* related back to Beethoven (his *No. 9*) and Mahler's perceived arrogance in emulating him by using a choir within a symphony. There was also the fact of the deaths of Beethoven, Bruckner and Schubert after each had composed nine symphonies – Mahler died after finishing his *No. 9*, leaving *No. 10* incomplete.

Near the conclusion of his study, Reik remembered an incident in which Mahler's father fantasized that his son would someday be a famous musician in Vienna. Reik's father had often spoken with great admiration of Mahler, leading to his son's appreciation of Mahler's music. Neither father lived to see his son's success.

Again, death intervened. Both Mahler and Abraham died at age 51; it was impossible for Reik to be released, to write *The Haunting Melody*, until after his 51st birthday.

References

1 Reik, T. *The Haunting Melody*. New York: Grove Press, pp. 222–224.
2 Mahler, G. *Symphony No. 2*. Mineola, NY: Dover, 1987, p. 379.
3 Reik, p. 252.

2

THEME: PART 2

Creativity

Theme: Part 1 dealt with a search for an answer to the question of why a particular piece of music affected the author, Theodor Reik. Reik had developed a relationship between a work of art and its creator, based upon the unconscious of one touching the unconscious of another. How does this work?

★

First, creativity in the arts is the manipulation and transformation of symbols . . . word, colour, shape, notes of music, etc. The artefact . . . a novel or poem, a painting or sculpture, a symphony . . . is the result of a completed process. In this section, I will trace the process that moves from artistic inspiration to finished product through the transformation of symbols. I will also reverse this process by considering the original coding in reverse, by decoding, in order to reach back into the mystery of inspiration. This will help us to understand the effect of the work of art in much the same manner as traced by Reik – the meaning of the melody that haunted him through an examination of his feelings about it. When the audience for a work of art becomes actively engaged, the inspiration transmitted is, ideally, the inspiration received.

Second, creativity is a mystery. As we seem to get closer to it, it begins to fade – finally disappearing. We attempt to approach it from different angles by leaping at it, or dropping upon it from above. Emptiness. It's not there. We're in the midst of . . . nothing. It doesn't exist.

But we know it does exist, not from its presence, but from what it leaves behind . . . residue/artistic artefacts. The reason it does not exist is because we have asked the wrong questions. Creativity *per se* is unknown; it is neither digital nor quantifiable.

I will discuss it from my own experience as a composer, as well as conversations I have had with several particularly articulate composers.

★

Something happens deep within my unconscious psyche. It could be sound, a vision or some combination of images. I am alerted in a manner that is difficult to describe beyond saying that I emotionally and physically feel its presence. Jung terms this 'instinctive energy'. It is a differentiated energy potential – with or without a profile at this state – archetypal. If I choose to develop this instinctive energy – this inspiration – into a musical composition, the process of symbolizing begins; it is striving to become known through entering consciousness.

Although I know this instinctive energy exists, I cannot begin to work it until I understand it; my method for achieving this understanding is to name it. There is always a descriptive word to attach. What is important at this point is that something – I will name it X – has been recognized as existing within my unconscious. This recognition allows me to begin the process of symbolic transforming. Through recognition of its existence, I have unconsciously translated an instinctive energy, an inspiration, into something I can creatively manage; this energy has become a symbol.

It is now necessary to change X into some communicable medium while retaining intact the symbol's essential qualities. As the process unfolds, these qualities begin to clarify themselves. A transduction into some artistic medium probably occurs simultaneously with the first transformation into a symbol. It is a natural thing for a creative artist to 'think' in terms of their own medium of expression. This language of articulation – the medium of artistic creation – is used to transmit X to others.

From recognition and symbolizing, through transduction into a medium, then outwards to consciousness – all are processes that move in symbols. I am assuming that we symbolize before consciously knowing. Otherwise, how could we be aware of something we do not know? With X providing the original energy, we can assume that the same symbol remains throughout the process, although it clearly becomes modified, elaborated and transformed.

To accomplish this process of transforming the symbol into an artefact that exists in consciousness requires the crossing of a threshold, into liminal space. It is in this space that X – translated, transduced, transformed – is ready for the conscious, ego-orientated processes of creativity, wherein experience, education and cultural viability take over; what has happened to us in our lives, what we have learned in school and what we have learned from others enable us to work the symbolic material into an artistic artefact.

However, there is one important step that must be taken. There is a barrier between consciousness and the unconscious; it is a censor that mediates those materials allowed to pass between them. The ego (consciousness) allows certain materials with which it cannot or does not want to deal to migrate into the unconscious, where those materials can remain for various durations. The unconscious migrates materials into consciousness through several pathways, such as dreams, symptoms, fairy tales and myths, and the creative arts.

Once through the censor, the symbol is consciously worked into an artefact. Jung understood that there would be differences between those works which ascend from the unconscious and those which merely begin from within a state of consciousness. He also realized that there would be a certain value attached to a work of art, in direct proportion to its success in bringing a symbol to life. As X is now being written in music notation (in my case), notions of the musical elements assume a position of importance. At this point, the choices of musical elements determine the configuration and shape of the symbol. The artefact, which now exists fully in consciousness, is completed, and is ready to be transmitted to an audience.

> *Once the conscious content has been given form and the meaning of the formulation is understood, the question arises as to how the ego will relate to this position, and how the ego and the unconscious are to come to terms. This is the second and more important stage of the procedure, the bringing together of opposites for the production of a third: the transcendent function.*[1]

The creative arts are a process of blending and reconciling a number of manipulations of a particular symbol into a completed artefact, a product of the transcendent function. The creative arts inform depth psychology.

These artefacts fall into two categories: those that require intermediaries/performers, and those that do not. In the former category are music (excluding electronic music), ballet and opera, films and plays; in the latter category are writings, art and sculpture.

In music, this artefact is given to symbol decipherers – performers – to translate into audible sounds. The use of intermediaries sometimes clouds one's perspective; are we listening to a great piece of music or a great performance of a piece of music . . . or both? Often with a conductor or performer who exhibits great physical charisma, we are actually watching what we hear.

The listener's experience is meant to be the same as the composer's – in reverse. This necessitates active engagement on the part of the listener. What was encoded in a particular order is now decoded in reverse order. The listener delves through the manifest content of the music, reaching for the latent content of the unconscious. X transmitted is, ideally, X received. Consciousness and the unconscious are no longer separate states, but areas along a continuum; in the creative arts, creator and perceiver move in either direction.

By assuming X as a 'message' from the unconscious, in later chapters of this book I will discuss a variety of creative artefacts that illustrate aspects of Jung's thinking, particularly those tensions that exist between opposites.

Reference

1 Jung, C. *The Transcendent Function*, in *Collected Works 8*, Para. 181.

3

THEME: PART 3

Freud and Mahler

I began with Reik's haunting by a section of Mahler's *Symphony No. 2*. Next, there was a brief study of the creative process, explaining the nature of that haunting in the emotional connection reached between the inspiration at the core of the symphony and the power it exerted on one particular listener, in Reik's case, and the audience in general, in the study of the process. I now move to an examination of the language used in psychological models, the semantics of which purport to enable us to move our discussion forward. In this third part of the theme we will discuss a meeting between Freud and Mahler, adding a fantasy account of what might have occurred had the meeting involved Jung and Mahler.

In 1910, a four-hour session occurred between Freud and Mahler. It was their only meeting. Mahler had recently learned of his wife Alma's infidelity. He was ill with heart disease from which he would die within six months. His conducting career in New York was not going well, reminiscent of the conclusion of his career in Vienna three years before. Although he had known of the heart disease for some time, the combination of issues had a profound influence on his emotional life.

However, simultaneously Mahler was working on *Symphony No. 10*, a work that, if finished, would have had an enormous influence on the music of the twentieth century, and beyond. The contrast of the two opposing forces of Mahler's anxiety and simultaneous creative breakthrough serves as a catalyst for added insight into a discussion of the language that we utilize in describing these forces. To do so, I shall briefly discuss the subject of Freud versus Jung. This is Freud's description of the Freud/Mahler session:

> *I analyzed Mahler for an afternoon in the year 1912 (or 1913?) in Leyden. If I may believe reports, I achieved much with him at that time. This visit appeared necessary to him, because his wife at the time rebelled against the fact that he withdrew his libido from her. In highly interesting expeditions through his life history, we discovered*

> *his personal conditions for love, especially his Holy Mary complex (mother fixation). I had plenty of opportunity to admire the capability for psychological understanding of this man of genius. No light fell at the time on the symptomatic façade of his obsessional neurosis. It was as if you would dig a single shaft through a mysterious building.*[1]

This is part of the letter that Freud wrote to his colleague, Theodor Reik. Freud also mentioned this meeting with Mahler to another colleague, Marie Bonaparte. Since their reports are similar, I assume that the points Freud discussed with them are as reported. In essence, a four-hour consultation yielded very little information; perhaps there was more that Freud decided to keep to himself.

Freud focused his attention on Mahler's family narrative, particularly his relationship with Alma, and Alma's relationship with her father. Much seems to have been made about an incident in Mahler's early life when he fled his parents' intense argument and, running into the street, heard a brass band performing music in the square outside his house, presumably militaristic music.

The quasi-militaristic nature of the music may have had some far-reaching identifiers with the atmosphere from which he ran, but the usual historically critical interpretations are that the incident formed the basis of Mahler's quick, non-motivated juxtaposition of dissimilar musics.

Some critics of the time had seized upon this musical stylistic feature as evidence of Mahler's inability to compose serious/great/profound music. Mahler apparently came away from the meeting with Freud feeling he had learned something about his own music, and was somehow relieved of guilt for amateurish musicality. He seems to have accepted musical criticism based upon psychoanalytic modelling. It was Mahler's acceptance of this displacement by Freud.

Critical to this issue is Freud's well-known lack of interest in and knowledge of music:

> *Freud himself never wrote specifically about music and his writings contain few references even of a metaphorical nature. Indeed, he appears to have been the least sensitive to music than any of the arts, an anomaly in late nineteenth century Vienna.*[2]

This does not excuse his inability to deal with Mahler's issues.

Another part of their session related to sexual behaviour. Freud criticized Mahler for having a wife so much younger than he; perhaps this was an explanation for Gustav and Alma's increasing lack of sexual intimacy. It is important to bear in mind that it was Gustav who lost his libido in reference to Alma rather than the reverse, which would seem immediately related to the age difference.

Photographs taken at the time show Mahler to be a seriously ill man. It is surprising that Freud made no reference to Mahler's obvious condition. Mahler had known about it since the time of his daughter's death in 1907. It was becoming worse. Was Mahler's denial so strong that the topic did not come up? Would it not have rated even a mention in Freud's communication with his colleagues?

Finally, there is reference to Mahler's obsessive behaviour, with no description of what that behaviour was. Mahler's concerns are translated into the word 'behaviour', named but not described: he is either ill or he isn't. This is language, but it is not science. It is a linguistic action whereby Freud puts Mahler in a position of *either/or*.

Family narrative – traumatic moment – sexual dysfunction – obsession: the points that Freud communicated to his colleagues. What Freud learned from Mahler was predictable. He condensed Mahler's conversation as if, in a sense, he was filling a shopping bag with life's mistakes, the choices of which validated his model of the mind. His thinking was convergent.

I have read about the Mahler/Freud session and its ramifications for many years, and have always found it puzzling. I will now construct a fantasy session, with Mahler and Jung; hopefully, this critique of the language used will clarify my concerns.

Jung often spoke of dealing with what is present in his patients. He would have constructed much of Mahler's narrative from incidents and feelings related to him by the anxiety-ridden composer; perhaps he would have Mahler walk into the anxiety. Starting in the present moment with Mahler, Jung would have intuited much about Alma and about Mahler's music. He would have discerned an unconscious psyche different from that discovered by Freud.

I would assume that early in their session Jung would have inquired about Mahler's dreams. Rather than taking several issues and condensing them inward as Freud had done, Jung would have used the symbols in the dream(s) to expand outward – breaking open the complexities from the inside. Jung's thinking was divergent, placing one in a position of *both/and*. Whatever was obstructing Mahler's psyche was in the present; the many disturbances were symptomatic, not symptoms.

Again: Mahler was close to death, his wife was unfaithful, etc. But . . . he was stepping into liminal space in the new encounters he was facing in *Symphony No. 10*. Yes, there were sudden musical changes in some of his music, but they were not a pathologized transference of a youthful trauma. They were one of the elements that have bound together and extended music for centuries; they were contrasts or, to use a term more meaningful in psychological reality, opposites. Mahler's use of musical contrast was certainly different from that of other composers, but it was a manifestation of his need to (re)create a universe that simultaneously led in many directions, rather than merely changing directions at times. This was one of the important aesthetic dimensions of his art. It was in no way indicative of an inferior technique.

Sometime during the conversation, Mahler's difficulties with Alma would probably have encompassed the revolution that was occurring within him. In the margins of *Symphony No. 10* Mahler wrote heart-rending messages and pleas to Alma. His discomfort regarding his future with Alma added to the artistic turmoil involved in creating the universe anew and would have, at the very least, aroused Jung's curiosity; music and Alma, and their symbiotic relationship, were the issues at hand.

Mahler probably would have briefly alluded to the difficulties with the new symphony. Jung's curiosity would have been triggered, and the question of whether or not this was a usual part of Mahler's compositional process would have been asked. This would have led Mahler back to his problem with *Symphony No. 2*, addressed earlier. This would follow with Jung inquiring about the results of that earlier confrontation with the creative cycle.

Thus, the discussion led to the phenomena at hand – the music . . . and Mahler as a musician. Had Mahler as music maker, *per se*, been in the forefront of the discussion, the shift in terms from contrast to opposite would have occurred. Critical thinking around 1910 was largely confounded by opposites, more so when contemplating their reconciliation. The opposites that were so intently discussed by Jung were theoretical, not clinical. Again, had Freud's interest in music or in the creative arts been greater, the discussion with Mahler would have been very different. Freud's distrust and lack of understanding of music was well known.[3] Freud also missed the symbiotic nature of Mahler's creations and their reflections of his love for Alma. But Freud is not alone in his lack of musical understanding.

There are two basic problems with much that has been written on the relationships between works of art and those who create them. First, there is a basic lack of understanding that music (e.g.) is a non-verbal linguistic form of communication. The most meaningful and precise quote I can offer is Susanne Langer's:

> *The content has been symbolized for us, and what it invites is not emotional response, but insight. 'Psychical Distance' is simply the experience of apprehending through a symbol what was not articulated before. The content of art is always real; the mode of its presentation, whereby it is at once revealed and 'distanced,' may be a fiction. It may also be music, or, as in the dance, motion. But if the content be the life of feeling, impulse, passion, then the symbols which reveal it will not be the sounds or actions that normally would express this life; not associated signs, but symbolic forms must convey it to our understanding.*[4]

Many others, including Koestler, Lévi-Strauss and Huxley have contributed to this construct. And from the musical community *per se*, Feder and Solomon have placed the dialogue on a different plateau.

Second, along with the lack of understanding of musical (and other non-verbal artistic) symbolic constructs, is the effort to mould aesthetic experiences into ordinary language. They do not fit into that mould. The mixing of neurosis and creativity is language-derived, but not part of the aesthetic experience.

If one considers the pathologized vocabulary of numerous studies linking the creative artist (and/or the genius) to neurosis or psychosis, it becomes clear that the early nineteenth-century stigma still prevails. Consider the use of the term 'obsession' in Freud's brief report of his meeting with Mahler: 'No light fell at the time on the symptomatic façade of his obsessional neurosis.'[5] What differentiates obsession from intense focus? Although they can be used interchangeably, one pathologizes while the other does not. When the artist is at work, they are intently focusing. The unconscious is being explored, and powerful emotions are being examined. The X from Chapter 2 is the operational principle.

Obsession is defined subjectively. It denotes a repetitive behaviour without change. In the scenario we are discussing, it is neurotic; there is no way to stop it, so it must continue. In no way does obsession define Mahler's creative behaviour. There were other matters that may be so defined, such as his continuing concerns with death, based upon a reality with which he lived for many years. But again – with so many deaths in his family, I think it not unusual to live with a certain feeling of fatality. However, I think it would exist in consciousness rather than in the unconscious psyche.

I suggest that the need to pathologize is a manifestation of the failure to understand the process of creativity. In a sense, this failure is a self-fulfilling prophecy; the arts are something powerful because they are challenging to the most profound aspect of emotion, and this type of emotional exploration is not understood . . . particularly by some in the psychological community. They must orient their thinking to an understandable concept. Thus, pathologize. To clarify: I am not speaking of the use of medical evaluation – pathologizing – in response to a symptom; rather, I am saying that the creative arts processes, *per se*, are not symptoms.

Although what we define as mental symptoms and the creative arts both emerge from the unconscious, confusion by classifying the arts in pathological language is, in itself, a symptom of nineteenth-century stigmatizing. It is a deduction from the language and its equivalent belief system under which we operate; it does not describe the artist or the artistic process.

Note that we used to, and largely still do, describe someone as *having* pneumonia but *being* depressed. Our language is indicative of our beliefs. 'Having' a disease means that some condition has entered from the outside, while 'being' something is existential, existing from the inside. For some illnesses the vocabulary is descriptive; for others, it's definitive. Descriptive/definitive – obsessed/intently focused. Captives of language, the mental illnesses of the creators themselves have become captives of linguistic oddities.

There is not only one model of the mind. The main question that I will ask throughout the following chapters is this: in working with the creative arts, is a model necessary? Is there any aspect of pre-conception on the part of psychology – the model – that matches the value and validity of the work of art itself? But besides the artists and the critics, who speaks meaningfully about the arts? Certainly, not those who impose a self-fulfilling vocabulary that merely evokes the image of the living art itself, without confronting the reality of the art.

Coda

The arts offer an alternate entrée into the psyche. Unlike the symbols that are the words of our everyday vocabulary, the arts speak to us in a different and unique gathering of symbols. These artistic symbols provide us a unique pathway to our unconscious psyche; the symbols of the creative arts originate and remain as direct access to our innermost being.

We feel the arts – we feel the emotions – they are beyond our language, and beyond the language that describes emotion. We must continue to look elsewhere . . . in addition to music, the additional arts.

Interlude

We begin our search for an understanding beyond language with a novel. Of course, we are dealing with words in contexts. But there are primary sources of energy, a rhizome, from which the created work emerges. There is a medium in which the work exists; in this case, it is time.

Some works of art are under the temporal control of the creator: music, dance, film, theatre. The audience accepts this. But even during those works where time is controlled by the audience – written and visual works – time plays an essential role. The movement of the eye while viewing a painting or reading a novel is under the control of the viewer. There are images and words that induce memory; this also is a use of time. Memory interrupts the flow of time, creating a different artefact.

Science conceives of time as linear: it is antecedent/consequent, cause/effect, unidirectional and continuous. Time is measurable and quantifiable. Thus, it is usable by science and is understood as the manner in which our biological lives flow.

But there is a different manner in which time flows; it is psychological and is the manner in which our mental and emotional lives flow. Our daily lives are continuous alterations and mixtures of past, present and future. There is no linearity.

In various ways, the creative arts control time; it is manipulated as part of the process. One can view the simultaneity of past/present/future by viewing a Cubist painting. Medieval painting gives us an undifferentiated view of time and space – viewing without spatial and temporal perspective.

Tender is the Night is a novel that deliberately confuses linear and psychological time, thus giving added importance to the use of memory.

References

1 Reik, T. *The Haunting Melody*. New York: Grove Press, 1953, p. 315.
2 Feder, S. 'Freud and music'. In M. Kelly (ed.), *The Encyclopedia of Aesthetics*. Oxford: Oxford University Press, p. 1. www.mindandmusic.org/feder_freud_music.html.
3 Reik, p. 315.
4 Langer, S. *Philosophy in a New Key*. New York: Mentor, 1942, p. 190.
5 Reik, p. 343.

4

TENDER IS THE NIGHT

In this chapter, I introduce the subject of time. As an undergraduate in one of Hans Meyerhoff's classes at UCLA, I remember him informing the class that Heraclitus said that you could never stand in the same river twice. Although it was not difficult to understand, the fluidity of time was a metaphor that has preoccupied me for decades. In the opening lines of *Four Quartets*, T.S. Eliot poses the issue of time in its scientific and poetically philosophical complexities.[1] Three brief notes illustrate Hans Meyerhoff's passage from the self, through literature, to time:

> *What we call the self, person, or individual is experienced and known only against the background of a succession of temporal moments and changes constituting his biography.*
>
> *The question, what is man, therefore invariably refers to the question of what is time.*
>
> *To be engaged in literature, therefore, quite naturally leads to questions about the meaning of time for the art form itself.*[2]

Jung, when introduced to the field of music therapy, opened a new linkage to music and stated, 'I feel that from now on music should be an essential part of every analysis. This reaches the deep archetypal work.'[3]

Langer and Kramer also firmly linked music with time: 'Music makes time audible'[4] and 'Music makes time meaningful'.[5]

Finally, an idea that has permeated the aesthetics of music for over a century: 'All art constantly aspires towards the condition of music',[6] which links music to all arts.

At first glance, it seems unusual to begin a discussion of a novel, *Tender is the Night*, with quotations on the subjects of time and music. I had chosen the first seven quotes when, for some unknown reason, I included the eighth. It presented itself unasked, directly from my unconscious, to this chapter. Such a powerful visitor required clarification; I decided to trace the quotation's origin in order to account for its presence. In a later chapter, I will have to account for this elevation into consciousness in an identical manner when I describe how the Mahler melody impinged upon Reik in *The Haunting Melody*.

In the creative arts, particularly music, time becomes not only audible and meaningful, but also memorable. Time and memory permit reciprocity among various aspects of the arts. The main point of Pater's idea seems to be that, while time is relevant in all art, whether the audience directs its own speed of perception (novels, poetry, painting, sculpture) or the speed is directed by the intermediary performer (music, ballet, theatre), music is the only art that cannot separate content and form. Temporal direction and/or words that describe feeling and, hence, tempo are attached to all musical notation. The symbols used in music are different from those used in common communication – words – and memory becomes an integral feature for understanding this art form. Without words and their ability to form referential thoughts, memory is called upon to create understanding. The imagination can move freely between past, present, and future, in any order. It is, therefore, somewhat incorrect to think that time cannot be recalled without limitation. For, in the creative arts – particularly music – there is a redeemable quality of time, which is memory. And it is the use of memory in the novel *Tender is the Night* that constantly strives to bring clarity to a rather complicated series of events. It is somewhat complicated to explain how musical/temporal symbols – musical notes and gestures performed in a time-controlled setting – bridge the gap to the language – the words – of *Tender is the Night*. The answer lies in the structure of the novel and the relationship of a 2–1–3 design, described below, to musical structures based upon non-linear memory. The following may be helpful in picturing what I am saying:

- Novel's structural order:
  Book 1, pp. 1–112;
  Book 2, pp. 115–235;
  Book 3, pp. 239–315
- Novel's temporal order:
  Book 2;
  Book 1;
  Book 3.

★

Non-linear temporal structures have often been used in the arts. Novels such as the *Alexandria Quartet* and *Remembrance of Things Past*, films such as *Memento* and *Rashamon*, music in Berlioz's *Symphonie Fantastique* and Wagner's *Ring*

Cycle all depend upon some redefinition of linear time – more lived than measured. They are similar in their use of memory.

Linear time simply means that the events of the narrative occur in one direction, the earliest to the latest. In non-linear time, the events do not flow in a unidirectional order, but one geared towards gaining the most psychological power. Thus, events that occur in different time periods are juxtaposed to illustrate their psychological importance.

The artistic use of non-linear time flow – the use of repetition of past events in the present – serves to bring both memory and expectation into the foreground, and to demonstrate that time is not unidirectional. Thus, we find that the 2–1–3 sequence is more powerful than the 1–2–3 would have been, because of the active temporal participation demanded of the audience. Not only must memory be shuffled, but expectation must be frustrated – leading, as Meyer suggests,[7] to emotional response. A musical example that closely follows Fitzgerald's temporal design is Elgar's *Enigma Variations*. I am referring to the placement of the dramatic moment located near the middle of the work rather than near the conclusion – an unusual placement in this period.

★

F. Scott Fitzgerald's *Tender is the Night* was published in 1934, nine years after *The Great Gatsby*. While the latter became a literary classic, the former was closer to Fitzgerald's soul. His inscription in a friend's copy of the book compared the two novels: *Gatsby* for its great writing and *Tender is the Night* for its powerful emotional content.[8]

What is meant by the power of emotion? It appears to be a simple, even simplistic, question. Ultimately, the answer to this question points to the pathway of understanding this great novel. In the search for the answer, I will consider the book from several perspectives: lived (psychological/non-linear) time versus measured (scientific/linear) time; the marriage of Dick and Nicole Diver as a fictionalized account of the marriage of Scott and Zelda Fitzgerald; the nature of appearance versus reality in the narrative; the use of Keats's *Ode to a Nightingale*, a quote that precedes the novel's beginning; and the subtle but recurrent attempts to recapture memory, based upon trust in the past that is the foundation of Romanticism.

If *Tender is the Night* had been written in linear time, the story would appear to be quite simple. However, the novel has a temporal sequence in which the events move from the middle (2) to the beginning (1) to the conclusion (3), yielding a linear sequence of 2–1–3 instead of the sequence 1–2–3 that would be expected.

The narrative (case history) in linear time: Dick Diver is a 26-year-old psychiatrist with a brilliant future. In 1917, he arrives in Zurich. He is there to see Nicole Warren, a girl in her late teens whom he had briefly met several years earlier. She is suffering from post-traumatic stress disorder, the result of an incestuous relationship with her father; she is later diagnosed as schizophrenic. After their first meeting, they had exchanged letters. Diver felt that Nicole was a maturing woman capable of benefiting from psychoanalysis.[9]

Nicole's doctor credits her improvement to Diver's interest in her. Diver becomes her doctor, her lover, her husband. Nicole is very wealthy; her fortune and her psyche under the control of her older sister, Baby. Baby wanted Nicole to marry a Chicago doctor, one who could both take care of her and provide respectable stability. Diver seemingly filled both roles.

After his marriage to Nicole, Dick writes psychiatric texts and, using Nicole's money, opens a clinic in partnership with her former doctor. They have two children and appear content: full participants in the generation of rich expatriates living in Europe after the Second World War. It is at this point in the novel's linear time that the novel begins. Fitzgerald places this background material, the personal history, in the middle of the novel. The important sources of the psychological background appear as the central focal point.

As the novel begins, we experience Dick and Nicole as the quintessence of the jazz age – the flapper generation: endless parties, dancing and drinking, non-communicative banalities in place of communication, non-committal sex. Everything is appearance; reality is a shadow. This clash of opposites between appearance and reality provides the background against which the ensuing drama is enacted. The continual sense of tension created by these opposites keeps the existential question continually in the forefront: is this reality?

Into this setting a young Hollywood starlet, Rosemary, arrives. Hollywood is the ultimate symbol of America's confusion between appearance and reality. In the third part of the novel, Rosemary and Dick develop a relationship which parallels that of Nicole and Dick: an initial, immediate attraction for Dick on Rosemary's part, with Dick later responding. By the time Rosemary and Dick become sexually involved, Nicole and Dick have become different persons. Dick has descended into alcoholic depression while Nicole has, seemingly, become increasingly self-confident. Patient and doctor have switched roles: the wounded is healed, the healer is wounded, or so it appears. The novel concludes: Rosemary is off to make a new movie, Nicole has taken a lover and Dick has lost interest in both his clinic and his wife. He returns to rural America to resume his life as a doctor.

The main relationship in the novel is that between Dick and Nicole Diver: doctor and patient at the novel's temporal beginning; husband and wife at the structural beginning. The roles have switched as a result of both Nicole's and Dick's failure to recognize the transference/countertransference that has occurred.

Dick did not attempt to end the relationship with Nicole at an early stage, when it could have been easily accomplished. To do so, he would have had to recognize the power of his countertransference. His realization of the presence of the countertransference led Dick to an appreciation of the freedom this recognition gave him.[10]

Seemingly, Dick understands his growing attachment to Nicole, and feels that he is in control. This allows him into a reality of expanding horizons, to study anew, and to build upon further achievements. The only problem he faces is that he doesn't have the funds for such a drastic change . . . without a private practice, one would assume.[11]

Rather than continue writing his academic book, Dick expresses a need to do something more to further his knowledge, something that would cost money. Dick is poor; Nicole is rich. A Faustian bargain emerges.

Another aspect questions Dick's sustained interest in Nicole: returning to the original meeting between Dick and Nicole and their exchange of letters, we realize that, in terms of mutual consciousness, neither is yet aware of what is occurring. Jung says:

> *The doctor, by voluntarily and consciously taking over the psychic sufferings of the patient exposes himself to the overpowering contents of the unconscious and hence to their inducting action . . . the patient, by bringing an activated unconscious content to bear upon the doctor, constellates the corresponding unconscious material in him, owing to the inducting effect which always emanates from projections to greater or lesser degree.*[12]

The 'healer' combines with the 'poor boy' within Dick to absorb their opposites: the 'wounded' and the 'rich' of Nicole. When projected onto each other, it might seem that the relationship would ideally form a union of these opposites, given the compensatory nature of what is being projected. But this assumption is based upon a belief that what is projected is received. This would also assume that the transference and countertransference, upon which the success of the analysis rests, would have worked. Jung points out a persistent danger:

> *The transference, however, alters the psychological stature of the doctor, though this is at first imperceptible to him. He too becomes affected, and has as much difficulty in distinguishing between the patient and what has taken possession of him as has the patient himself. This leads both of them to a direct confrontation with the daemonic forces lurking in the darkness.*[13]

In spite of the absorbing of one another's projections, the union of opposites between the two failed, because the conscious awareness of the unconscious, either of oneself or of the other, was not present in either of them. Nor was empathy present, based upon reality rather than appearance. The ability to actually understand what was being communicated to each of them by the other was, for different reasons, not present. In common was the issue that neither could absorb the painful reality from the other that was beyond his/her ego development. To more completely understand this, we must extend the narratives of Dick and Nicole to those of Scott and Zelda Fitzgerald.

In most ways, Dick and Nicole are Scott and Zelda. The main outlines in the lives of the two couples, one in appearance and the other in reality, are remarkably similar. This was neither the first nor last time that Fitzgerald used events from his and Zelda's lives as models for his work.

A close friend of the Fitzgerald's, Gerald Murphy, who was mourning the recent death of one of his children and the critical illness of the other, wrote to Scott concerning *Tender is the Night*:

> *I know that what you said in 'Tender is the Night' is true. Only the invented part of our life, the unreal part – has any scheme of beauty. Life itself has stepped in now and blundered, scarred and destroyed. In my heart, I dreaded the moment when our youth and invention would be attacked in our only vulnerable spot – the children, their growth, their health, their future.*[14]

Murphy clearly distinguished between the 'true' and the 'unreal', and must have been attempting to make Scott aware of the novelist's vulnerability.

Fitzgerald used the Murphys' tragedy, which is symbolized as the death of innocence for Dick/Scott and the wounding of Murphy's wife, Sara/Zelda, or perhaps the subversion of the 'faith' referred to earlier. (This scenario is similar to that of Gustav and Alma Mahler after the death of their child.) For Dick, the separation from his children at the end of the book in an emotionally profound scene – a scene drawn from Murphy's letter – is a powerful representation of innocence lost. It is the most powerful expression of feeling in the novel,[15] similar in many ways to an equally powerful scene in Tim Winton's *The Riders*, Chapter 15. In both examples, Pater's comment on all arts seeking the condition of music seems appropriate when considering some of the powerful moments that certain pieces of music have brought us, particularly when associated with words. When immersed in an overpowering feeling, we often share that space with other, simultaneous types of input – the arts combining Dick's/Scott's loss of innocence, being able to embrace the reality of life ultimately leads to the downfall of the marriage. Instead of facing his shadow, the necessity of which was dictated by Nicole's seeming independence, he became an alcoholic, engaging in a compensatory movement of self-anaesthetization. The sterility of his life, resulting from the Faustian bargain, was left unexamined until the affair with Rosemary. But that affair, too, proved ephemeral. In the last section of the novel, his slow and painful separation from Nicole cleared the way for his integration of the past, and ultimately to his individuation. Appearance has been replaced by reality; he had no life.

How did Dick survive? Given the dissolution of everything meaningful in his life, even including the nihilism of the times, it would have been appropriate for Dick to have been destroyed, much as was Gatsby. Fitzgerald offered an explanation and additional insight into Dick's survival in the chronicle of his own alcoholic disintegration in his essay 'The Crackup', dealing with the tension of opposites.[16]

Consider Jung on this subject:

> *The repressed content must be made conscious so as to produce a tension of opposites without which no forward movement is possible. The conscious mind is on top, the*

shadow underneath, and just as high always longs for low, and hot for cold, so all consciousness, perhaps without being aware of it, seeks its unconscious opposite, lacking which it is doomed to stagnation, congestion, and ossification. Life is born of the spark of opposites.[17]

What does it mean to hold this tension of opposites in one's mind? For our purposes, it means something that ignites the spark of creativity, the activation of X. Both Fitzgerald and his fictional counterpart Diver are writers . . . possessors of the spark.

All of the real issues between Scott and Zelda were fictionalized into Dick and Nicole. The Divers were the Fitzgeralds; one can move from novel to real life and back again with ease. What are found are the narratives of two women played out against the background of their husbands . . . and their fathers.

Nicole and Zelda sought to integrate those parts of themselves from which they had been forced to retreat: Zelda's creativity in its fictionalized format was Nicole's quest for individuation. In these two cases the women surrendered control of critical parts of their psyches by projecting onto the apparent Dick and the real Scott their struggles. But neither Dick nor Scott was capable of accepting these projections; Nicole and Zelda had to attempt to refocus upon themselves. The inability to receive was of equal importance in the dissolution of the real and fictionalized relationships. In Scott's construction, Dick would eventually realize that, as the novel's structure illuminates, he must return to his past to recoup his soul . . . the soul of Romanticism.

Lack of integration was demonstrated by a severe imbalance of opposites, physically symbolized by symptoms of alcoholism, depression and finally – in Zelda's case – the reality of schizophrenia. These opposites were psychologically manifested by the cluttered confusion between appearance and reality of both people and events. The liberating spark of creativity could not be ignited. Scott was well aware of his role in this; in a letter to one of Zelda's doctors, he wrote:

In the last analysis she [Zelda] is a stronger person than I am. I have creative fire but I am a weak individual. She knows this and really looks upon me as a woman. All our lives, since the days of our engagement, we had spent hunting for some man Zelda considers strong enough to lean upon. I am not.[18]

Fitzgerald's attempts to solve the problem of his weakness included the creations of both Gatsby and Diver; Dick was the healer that Scott could never be and, in appearance, Gatsby was the power that eluded Dick. Neither of them was strong enough to be the man that Zelda/Nicole needed. Their overwhelming weakness was the profound lack of empathy for women. What was being asked of the man was an understanding of the animus in woman, but also a plea for acknowledging the anima in man; this latter involved the understanding of the projection spoken of above. Nicole did not exist in the mould in which Dick perceived her; the healer had not healed. At the conclusion of *Gatsby*, Fitzgerald reflects upon the appearance of Daisy's green light, his acceptance of it as a reality, but ultimately realizing that his quest has not yet ended.[19]

In *Tender is the Night*, Fitzgerald offered a different solution. Dick Diver does not die. Symbolically integrating his past by returning to it, he integrates *Gatsby*'s last lines, returning to America once again to become a healer.

The integration of the ending of *Gatsby* and Diver's return to his past provide me with the transition back to the temporal element of this novel. Earlier, I suggested that non-linear time produced an involvement on the part of the audience that, by emphasizing memory, creates a powerful effect: closure expected, then frustrated, finally reached – the main thesis of Meyer:

> *Emotion or affect [in music] is aroused when a tendency to respond is arrested or inhibited.*[20]

Manipulation of time moulded vitality into the content. But Fitzgerald's use of this technique is different from that of others. Elements of a cyclic structure are apparent in novels by Proust and Durrell, free association in Joyce and in film by Kurasowa. In an article on Renais' remarkable film *Last Year at Marienbad*, Dave Kehr begins with this quote from another important filmmaker of the time, Jean-Luc Godard:

> *'A film should have a beginning, a middle and an end, but not necessarily in that order.' But Mr. Renais put the theory into practice. Composed of lines of dialogue repeated with slight shifts in emphasis, scenes restaged from different angles or with actors in different positions – all embedded within lengthy tracking shots through the baroquely overdecorated corridors of the hotel or its eerie formal gardens (where the human figures cast a shadow, but the shrubs and statuary do not) – 'Marienbad' seems to be taking place simultaneously in the past, present, and future.*[21]

Here we have an artistic enactment very close to the content of Eliot's poem mentioned at the beginning of this chapter.

Elgar's *Enigma Variations* is a musical example which follows the intention of the temporal design of *Tender is the Night.* All works in the generic theme and variations format first present a theme that is taken through a series of alternations and elaborations, depending upon the style period. Although Elgar's theme is presented quietly at the work's beginning, it appears in a full-blown dramatic setting in the ninth (Nimrod) variation – at about the work's mid-point. As in Fitzgerald's novel, the generating source of the music upon which all else is built, particularly in its dramatic sense, appears at the mid-point in the linear time flow. This 2–1–3 temporal design is used to create a different type of linearity, one that moves from present, to the past, and then continues with the opening present. Memory has become a generating force. But why? How did Fitzgerald's muse bring him to Keats's poem *Ode to a Nightingale*?

Fitzgerald's generation was the product of scientific revolutions, the beginnings of psychoanalysis and its focus on the unconscious, the revolutions of governments and social structures, the questioning of religion – the very essences of reality being redefined. Fitzgerald's culture was that of the flappers: laughter, dancing, drinking and sexual promiscuity. To be caught in the midst of this overlap, with the world changing, could feel like a maelstrom; to be riders within the maelstrom is certainly enough to create some varieties of existential trauma, even pathology. What, then, would have been the purpose of Fitzgerald's contrasting of linear versus psychological time that permeates the motivations of his characters?

★

As to the idea of faith in its non-religious sense, which Dick included in the inscription to his friend: he had made the Faustian bargain, translated into a non-empathic healer. Within the chosen container of his marriage to Nicole, he failed in his attempts at being a healer, husband and man – a product of Scott. But the critical feature was the attempt, not the failure. The spark of creativity was the strongest force within Scott; it served as a testament to faith in the essential goodness of man, based upon the reality of past Romanticism rather than the appearance, the maelstrom of the present and thus predictable future. The archetype that Scott contacted was the real past – it was, in fact, Romanticism. He was romantically in love with the metacharacter of Zelda and her persona. According to Trilling:

> *Fitzgerald was perhaps the last notable writer to affirm the Romantic fantasy, descended from the Renaissance, of personal ambition and heroism, of life committed to, or thrown away for, some ideal of self.*[22]

Fitzgerald prefaced his novel with this quote from Keats's *Ode to a Nightingale*:

Already with thee! Tender is the night . . .
. . . But here there is no light,
Save what from heaven is with the breezes blown
Through verdurous glooms and winding mossy ways.

The voice I hear this passing night was heard
In ancient days by emperor and clown:

Adieu! adieu! thy plaintive anthem fades,
Past the near meadows, over the still stream,
Up the hill-side; and now 'tis buried deep
In the next valley-glades;
Was it a vision, or a waking dream?
Fled in that music: – do I wake or sleep?[23]

In the act of creation, Fitzgerald sought transcendence, his vision and longing being guided by breezes from heaven and the passing voice of the poet-nightingale. In *Healing Fiction*, Hillman addresses the concept of the creative arts:

> *We respond to painting and music without translation, why not as well the dream? Imaginative art forfeits interpretation and calls instead for a comparable act of imagination.*[24]

Dick Diver, the Faustian archetype having made his bargain, and through an act of courage a memorial to his past, attempted to reverse his decision . . . to travel back to his future. At the novel's conclusion, Dick finally became a hero, his journey completed. It was Fitzgerald's faith in the act of creation that made certain that the passing voice of the poet would be heard.

Interlude

Incorporating a discussion of time, of necessity, requires us to consider the manifestations of memory in this context. Psychological time is the framework in which memory exists. It is through the characters in the narrative that the temporal issues become meaningful. The psychological archaeology of the narrative brings us in proximity to the unconscious psyche. Indeed, 'archaeology' is a method for investigating time past, and incorporating that study into the present.

As we uncover various aspects of the narrative's past, we inevitably confront the issue of opposites – to which we now turn our attention.

References

1 Eliot, T.S. 'Burnt Norton'. *Four Quartets*. New York: Harcourt Brace & Company, 1971, p. 13.
2 Meyerhoff, H. *Time in Literature*. Berkeley and Los Angeles, CA: University of California Press, 1960, pp. 1–3.
3 McGuire, W. and Hull, R. (eds). *C. G. Jung Speaking*. Princeton, NJ: Princeton University Press, 1977, p. 275.
4 Langer, S. *Feeling and Form*. New York: Scribner, 1953, p. 110.
5 Kramer, J. *The Time of Music*. New York: Schirmer, 1988, p. 1.
6 Pater, W. *The Renaissance: Studies in Art and Poetry*. Mineola, NY: Dover, p. 90.
7 Meyer, L. *Emotion and Meaning in Music*. Chicago and London: University of Chicago Press, 1956.
8 Scott Fitzgerald, F. *Tender is the Night*. New York: Scribner, 1986, p. XV.
9 Ibid., p. 121.
10 Ibid., p. 146.
11 Ibid.
12 Jung, C. *The Practice of Psychotherapy, Collected Works 16*, Para. 364.
13 Ibid., Para. 375.
14 Taylor, K. *Sometimes Madness is Wisdom: Zelda and Scott Fitzgerald, A Marriage*. New York: Ballantine, 2001, p. 307.

15 Scott Fitzgerald, p. 311.
16 Scott Fitzgerald, F. 'The crack-up'. *The Jazz Age*. New York: New Directions, 1996, p. 55.
17 Jung, C.G. *On the Psychology of the Unconscious, Collected Works* 7, Para. 78.
18 Taylor, pp. 257–258.
19 Scott Fitzgerald, F. *The Great Gatsby*. New York: Scribner, 1953, p. 180.
20 Meyer, p. 14.
21 Kehr, D. 'Incredible '60s memories'. *New York Times*, 12 June 2009, p. AR13.
22 Trilling, L. *The Liberal Imagination*. New York: Doubleday, 1948, p. 242.
23 Cook, E. (ed.). 'Ode to a Nightingale'. *John Keats: The Major Works*. Oxford: Oxford University Press, 2001.
24 Hillman, J. *Healing Fiction: On Freud, Jung, Adler*. Dallas, TX: Spring, 1983, pp. 29–30.

5

INGMAR BERGMAN'S *PERSONA*

Beginning this chapter on *Persona*, something caused me to pause. I was reflecting upon *Tender is the Night* and then back to the chapter on *The Haunting Melody*. The question that was causing such unease was not one of content, but of structure: Reik's in his book and mine in my chapter.

The idea intruded upon me, a remembrance of the uncertainty, coupled with excitement, when I first read Durrell's *Alexandria Quartet*. Upon reading it, I found the answer to why I was pausing, clearly articulated by Durrell in the two quotes below, and back into Reik's book. I realized that I have assumed the 'technique' of sliding panels, superimposed upon the personal archaeology of Reik's journey – which becomes clear in the final few chapters of this book.

Structure and time are basic to all arts, and will be referred to frequently. A few examples from the *Alexandria Quartet*:

> *Pursewarden's idea of a novel of 'sliding panels' . . . or else like some medieval palimpsest where different sorts of truth are thrown down one upon the other . . .*[1]

> *. . . I had set out once to store, to codify, to annotate the past before it was utterly lost . . . no sooner had I embalmed one aspect of it in words than the intrusion of new knowledge disrupted the frame of reference, everything flew asunder, only to reassemble again in unforeseen, unpredictable patterns . . .*[2]

These aspects of time, and structure, we revisit in other chapters.

I view *Persona* not as a static, completed work, but as a continuing work-in-progress. But, of course, it is I who am in progress and the reader who is witness to this process of placing events in the past and present, simultaneously. It is partially my past of which I speak, and the choices it dictates to the present – this book. I was recently reminded of this while reading Robert Romanyshyn's *The Wounded*

Researcher.[3] For me, the next part of his title is critical: 'Research with the Soul in Mind'. The passage I read was a quote: 'There is only the fight to recover what has been lost and found, and lost again and again.'[4] *Four Quartets* is the poem I mentioned at the beginning of Chapter 4. I was reading Romanyshyn's book after completing the *Alexandria Quartet.* Obviously the panels are sliding.

★

A montage of visual images occurs at the beginning of *Persona.* They are in abbreviated form at the film's conclusion, and at the film's mid-point. The sequence begins with a film projector gone awry, followed by images of a cartoon, hands, a film clip of a skeleton in a comedic role, bleeding sheep's organs, white light, a nail being driven into a hand, a painting of trees that morph into real trees, a spiked fence, dirt, rocks, a dead person, a boy under a sheet, a dangling hand of a corpse, dead people in a morgue, a ringing phone, a boy putting on his glasses and reading – touching a huge screen upon which a woman's face appears. This last image becomes increasingly important as the film progresses and we realize that the woman is Elizabeth Vogler in her persona and the rejecting, or in Cater's formulation, the negative mother.[5]

All of the images have symbolic content that unfolds throughout the film. For this chapter, the most important are the projector and the image of the boy reaching for the image on the screen. Music also has a significant role in emphasizing significant structural points. While it is tempting to connect these points into a musical structure *per se*, it is a necessary point to make. The music is simple, emphatic and perfectly appropriate to the dramatic content. (Bergman's last film, *Saraband*, is an excellent example of a film's formal structure derived from a music/dance form.)

The visual images that are musically highlighted occur at critically dramatic points: the beginning and ending plus three powerful mid-points. The first of these mid-points occurs near the film's beginning. Elizabeth is lying in the hospital. Alma has just reflected upon her uncertainty of being able to nurse her. Elizabeth is listening to Bach. She turns to the radio, focusing her attention on it; she cries. The music has stirred some memory. But what may this memory be?

Although there is no direct connection to the other music in the film, mainly created by Lars Johan Werle, Bach has a very close connection to Bergman himself. Similar to the stimulus of the word 'faith' in the previous chapter, the question arises, 'why Bach?' or perhaps even 'why Bergman?'. This serves as a catalyst to our curiosity regarding Bergman's insertion of himself into this film . . . soon discussed in detail.

The second musical point occurs when Elizabeth is looking at a picture of Nazis threatening a Jewish child in the Warsaw ghetto. The musical gesture is a chord built from instrumental colours evolving from within the sonority: evolving colours in motion within pitch choices that are static – unmoving. Motion versus stasis: incredible tension results.

The third musical point coincides with the film's most striking moment – the blending of the faces of Alma and Elizabeth into one face. When the opening image of the boy reaches for the screen image, whom we now intuit to be his mother, the film concludes, the music ends . . . the projector stops. Dramatic underscoring is the reason for the music's importance. It is, however, the visual imagery that articulates the film's structure. They are so closely integrated that both serve Bergman's narrative and how he wishes to be understood.

The dramatic mid-point occurs when the film briefly breaks into images from the film's beginning, and later its ending. At this mid-point, Bergman adds a searching eye ('I?') to the image. Alma has just read Elizabeth's letter to her psychiatrist, the impact of which eventually results in Alma's loss of self-control. Alma confronts Elizabeth with this thought: 'I always thought that artists are compassionate, that they create out of compassion.'

Alma feels betrayed. She must conclude that the persona that Elizabeth, the artist, presents is fake. Bergman's use of the searching eye adds to the moment's importance. A question is being posed: is it the meaning of art, or of Bergman's place in the world of art, that is being highlighted? In another formulation: is Bergman dealing with the women's persona, or his own?

The opening images present an unusual blending; they are without direction or sequencing. In some sense, they are opposites: life and death; whole and detached/wounded body parts; appearance and reality; comedy and death, spikes on a fence and in a hand, and projector and its image – a more sophisticated form of appearance and reality. The blending of the women's faces will become the central image, thus reconciling opposites in the most direct fashion. This blending eventually raises the question of whether we are looking at two separate psyches or two aspects of one psyche.

Some have speculated that Bergman's usage of the visual images is self-reflexive. The technique – one of obvious use of symbolism – draws attention to the film, filmmaking *per se*, and by extension to the filmmaker, to Bergman as 'auteur'. This quality is suggested by Steene,[6] Sontag[7] and Orr.[8] Although such a description serves to place Bergman within the context of filmmakers of the 1960s, it draws attention to the content, an issue addressed by McLuhan.[9] It obscures the relationship between the visual images of opposites and their counterpart in the film – the women's blending. For McLuhan, 'the medium is the message' is a way of saying that the conduit precedes the content in importance. With Bergman as auteur for his striking use of visual images, conduit trumps content. But if the speculation is mainly influenced by Bergman's actual role in *Persona*, if he is actually present, then content trumps conduit – the latter in service to the former.

The actress Elizabeth Vogler becomes mute in the midst of a performance of *Electra*. Lacan points out that *Electra* is in certain ways the very double of *Antigone* – 'Dead in life, I am already dead to everything,' she says.[10] Sontag also uses the term 'doubling', in her case to refer to repetition leading to transformation.[11] Lacan and Sontag bring to mind the Durrell quote from the beginning of the chapter – the 'sliding panels', the 'palimpsest'. The transformation that is manifest in

Elizabeth's symptomatic selective mutism may be her collective grief (Vietnam *et al.*) or her personal grief (her child) – or both.

At a critical point in Sophocles' play, Electra's mother Clytemnestra says: 'There is a strange power in motherhood; however terrible her wrongs, a mother never hates her child.'[12] The distancing of the negative mother towards her child is an opening and closing image of the film, where the child is unable to reach her. Elizabeth finds her child repulsive, and rejects him . . . powerful material for her unconscious psyche . . . her shadow. However, Bergman says that Elizabeth's silence is not to be taken as a psychotic symptom. Rather, he conceived of it as a strong protest against society. The event immediately preceding her mutism was a TV news clip showing a Buddhist priest's self-immolation.

Sontag's use of the term 'doubling' adds complexity to the discussion. In Rank's book[13] on the subject of doubling, an early example of a psychoanalytic approach to film analysis, he focuses on guilt, identity and, particularly, on narcissism – a usage consistent with Bergman's conception. Sontag adds:

> *In my own view, the construction of* Persona *is best described in terms of this variations-on-a-theme form. The theme is that of doubling; the variations are those that follow from the leading possibilities of that theme (on both a formal and psychological level) such as duplication, inversion, reciprocal exchange, unity and fission, and repetition. The action cannot be univocally paraphrased. It's correct to speak of* Persona *as relating the duel between two mythical parts of a single self: the corrupted person who acts (Elizabeth) and the ingenuous soul (Alma) who founders in contact with corruption.*[14]

(I am perplexed by Sontag's musical analogy. It feels as if she is searching for a musical idea that would correspond to her literary analysis. If a musical structure is to be used, the more appropriate one would be sonata rondo, where the main idea structurally recurs, with variations serving as a kind of development.) As I said earlier, the idea of a musical structure derived from this film is a weak one. But this does not invalidate the importance of the musical underscoring.

Considering Elizabeth's self-inflicted distancing from her child, the attendant world issues illustrated from Vietnam and the Holocaust, I would suggest that Jung's concept of the shadow is a more complete formulation:

> *The shadow is a moral problem that challenges the whole ego-personality, for no one can become conscious of the shadow without considerable moral effort. To become conscious of it involves recognizing the dark aspects of the personality as present and real.*[15]

These aspects that the ego needs to avoid are hidden: sometimes unknown, sometimes repressed; sometimes personal, sometimes part of the collective. We are dealing with Elizabeth's dual avoidances of her maternal rejection and the horrors of war – both moral problems.

Some consider Elizabeth's silence to be passive-aggressive. Manifestly, this is so, but such an easily pathologized description yields little. Yes, this is how she behaves . . . but why? Elizabeth's psychiatrist dismisses her patient's motives, and takes a position that she terms 'beyond psychology'. John Simon is explicit:

> *Thus, her condition may be caused by the inflamed world, the cooling of the flesh, or by an artful devil within, a devil connected with her art.*[16]

I don't quite understand the use of 'devil' in her art. Does it refer to Elizabeth's position in the world of art, not as a Freudian neurosis but as a container for the artist's point of view? It is a psychotic world, but is it the visible images that cause the symptoms? Not incidentally, these images are Bergman's chosen medium; they are catalysts for Elizabeth's symptom, something obviously buried within her unconscious psyche.

Alma is a product of Swedish society, with which Bergman was constantly at war. She is looking forward to job, marriage and children with no particular passion: smug and self-confident. All of her Swedish certainties collide with the uncertainties produced by Elizabeth's silence. The contrast between Alma's constant talking and Elizabeth's silence is powerful. It is also compensatory. Each gives what the other needs. Bergman has created an extreme tension between these opposites, and much of the film's power derives from the need for reconciliation, which occurs in the blended scene discussed below.

The relationship between Alma and Elizabeth, both emotional and physical, is the manifest focus of *Persona*. Although the balance may be continually shifting in this set of opposites, it remains a relationship of the wounded and the healer, as in Chapter 4. At the point of reconciliation – the blended faces – it moves beyond the personal into an archetypal image.

Sexuality and motherhood are painful parts of both Alma's and Elizabeth's personal histories. Elizabeth became pregnant on a whim, in response to criticism directed at her at a party; someone suggested that she was incomplete without being a mother. After she became pregnant, she realized it was a mistake, but for some unspecified reason it was too late for an abortion. She finds her child repulsive, but also feels guilty for her inability to mother him. This is the image from the opening, of the boy reaching out to the woman on the screen. Her husband is quite a bit older than she, but there is no information regarding a daughter–father issue. Although he professes his love for her, she demonstrates no interest in or affection for him. Her flesh has been 'cooled', assuming it was ever otherwise.

Alma also became pregnant, as a result of a highly erotic encounter with a young boy – or perhaps with her fiancé. She did abort her foetus, and later experienced feelings of guilt. She seemed unable to understand what had happened; pregnancy placed her highly controlled plans for the future in jeopardy. 'How can you be two people at once?' she asks, meaning prudish and sensual. She gave up the erotic for the dull and predictable. The self-satisfied healer was deeply wounded.

In common are Alma's and Elizabeth's sexuality, repressed as a result of their choice of the men in their lives. They also feel a guilt regarding children. Nonetheless, there is a strong sexual current between them. Whether they actually have sex with each other is unclear. They are each the libido's shadow of the other, attested to by the nature of their emotional entanglement. In one important scene, later repeated, the two women enact Munch's *Vampire.* The hair of Elizabeth is wrapped around Alma – literally entangling her. Like the Munch painting, it is difficult to ascertain if this is a scene of vampirism or of sexual contact . . . or both.

Michels[17] believes this scene to be evocative of the 'vampire subgenre'. It occurs twice: first, just after Alma has related details of her erotic beach encounter causing her to become hysterical and Elizabeth to comfort her – the exchange of wounded/healer positions; and, second, immediately after Alma finally succeeds in getting Elizabeth to speak one word: 'ingenting' (nothing). In exchanging roles, the women have switched personae. It is as if each was a fragment of the shadow, or double, of the other.

> *The persona is a complicated system of relations between individual consciousness and society, fittingly enough a kind of mask, designed on the one hand to make a definite impression upon others, and, on the other, to conceal the true nature of the individual.*[18]

The function of the mask is to separate the individual's appearance from reality. As the vampire scenes illustrate, both appearance and reality can change while the mask remains in place. Perhaps the two women, the sliding panels, are interchangeable parts of a whole, and the roles they play are not separate people at all, but pieces of a single human psyche.

> *What goes on behind the mask is then called 'private life.' This painfully familiar division of consciousness into two figures, often preposterously different, is an incisive psychological operation that is bound to have repercussions on the unconscious.*[19]

The idea of divided qualities within one woman has been used by Munch in his painting *Woman in Three Stages*, and by Reik in his essay on Offenbach's *The Tales of Hoffmann.*[20]

Another differentiation is that between ego and persona – between internal necessities and external demands:

> *We have to discover that we use our representational clothes for protection and appearance but that we can also change into something more comfortable when it is appropriate and can be naked at other times. If our clothes stick to us or seem to replace our skin we are likely to become ill.*[21]

More directly:

> *To the extent that ego-consciousness is identified with the persona, the neglected inner life (personified in the shadow and anima or animus) is activated in compensation. The consequences, experienced in symptoms characteristic of neurosis, can stimulate the process of individuation.*[22]

Persona, shadow, compensation . . . and now anima and individuation. How do these draw together in Bergman's film?

Progoff opens a discussion of the film with the idea that 'Bergman had intuitively recognized the principles of depth psychology and was applying them in his work'; he quotes Bergman, 'all my pictures are dreams'.[23] Expressed in the creative arts, Bergman has intuitively grasped the concept of compensation expressed through symbols within dreams.

The anima is the inner feminine side of a man.[24] Archetypes of anima and shadow appear in fragments. They may be in dreams, in reveries or simply when working through an idea. Since these fragments appear in the unconscious psyche, it is up to consciousness to decipher the coded symbols. As I suggested earlier, the created artefact, in this case the film, is the realization of the journey from the unconscious.

From the opening and closing images of *Persona*, we have noted the child (Bergman) reaching for his mother . . . his anima. The film becomes a vehicle for Bergman attempting to understand this process of individuation. If the film were analysed from a story board, one could capture the temporal scheme in its entirety, without the interruptions of repetition. Bergman's presence would be strongly felt. But we are dealing with psychological time, the time of the creative arts.

Elizabeth and Alma are incomplete fragments who, when their faces are blended together, are realized as his anima: they complement each other and, as a whole, complement Bergman. What his critics labelled 'auteur' is, in reality, an artist on his journey of self-discovery.

Jung points out that 'we call the unconscious "nothing" and yet it is a reality *in potentia*'.[25] At the moment of uttering 'ingenting', Elizabeth's mutism begins to vanish. This mutism was her shadow; a manifestation of the perils of the soul. For Elizabeth, these perils consisted of Vietnam and the Holocaust; for Alma, the peril consisted of her failure with Elizabeth, which violated her self-contained world. These societally enforced contents of their respective unconscious psyches demonstrated the possible repercussions: Elizabeth's silence and Alma's constant talk, which were not only symptoms but also fragments that were complementary to one another, and compensatory for Bergman's film. For it is his actual appearance at the film's conclusion, plus the interjections of the projector at three points, which states: This is me.

I have often wondered why Bergman did not pursue the well-known symbol of the Janus face to portray the relationship between the two women. Janus would have shown the two women as connected but separate, and the ego-consciousness would dominate. But the blended image delineates a symbolic whole – two personae in one. This whole, whose construction is the integrated opposites, is the completed anima sought by Bergman. His anima is the persona of the film. While we know that the face on the opening and closing screen images is that of his mother, we also could be aware that it is the face of Liv Ullmann, who will eventually play an important role in Bergman's real life.

In Durrell's study of the many faces of love, the vision that begins his journey is that of Justine. The vision that signifies the end of his journey, and the beginning of a new one, is Clea. The foundation of the palimpsest is both a conclusion and a guide to the future. For Bergman, *Persona* is precisely that kind of film. It is fitting that his choice of communicating his vision is the projector.

Coda: *Saraband*

In the two preceding chapters, I have followed a single thread as it gradually led to a conclusion. In Chapter 4, the meaning of Fitzgerald's use of time led me to an understanding of the word 'faith', and to how Romanticism was the operative force; the focus on the past was to highlight those aspects of life during those times that were of particular value to Dick Divers – particularly love and the creative forces that it engenders. In Chapter 5, issues of doubling, splitting, mutism and anima/animus separations raised the question of Bergman's recurring presence, in several forms, and what their purpose may have been.

Although music was mentioned in both chapters, its contribution was indirect: the aesthetics of structural design in *Tender is the Night*, and its underscoring of narrative highpoints in *Persona*. This discussion of Bach's *Saraband* brings music into a direct relationship with the structure and content of the film. An understanding of the music yields threads of information, which open pathways to understanding the film. I have already touched upon Bergman's devotion to the music of Bach; *Saraband* allows us to follow Bergman's journey from his unconscious psyche, guided by Bach, through the completion of the film.

Why did Bergman choose Bach's *Cello Suite No. 5/Saraband* as the focal point for this film? The Saraband was a part of the sixteenth-century dance suite, occurring just before the concluding dance. It is slow, quiet and stately, serving as an upbeat to the dramatic closing gig, a faster and more energetic dance. And this is the way in which it is used in the film. The *Saraband* is only performed once in the foreground. Karin and Henrik have just had the most dramatic confrontation in the film; Karin is seen performing the work with Henrik looking on, stricken with grief and fear of Karin's leaving him. The following two dialogues in the film (9 and 10) are less intense; the format is the same as in Bach's *Suite*, except that the dramatic roles are reversed; the consistent element is the contrast of successive sections – *the* aesthetic principle of the Baroque epoch.

The dance suite was composed for instruments, but the individual dances had vocal ancestries from the Renaissance. This particular movement, Bach's *Saraband*, exemplifies this vocal ancestry. One need only listen to the *Crucifixus* of Bach's

Mass in B Minor to understand the vocal derivation of the cello piece. I suggest that it could have been the textless but mournful quality of the *Saraband*'s opening phrase that attracted Bergman as a foundation for his film.

In an interview, Bergman described *Saraband* as ten dialogues preceded by a prologue and concluded with an epilogue. The dialogues are numbered and titled in the film. Each has two characters. The opening phrase of Bach's piece has one theme clearly divided into two equal phrases: the first is harmonically less stable than the second, and this first descends while the second ascends. They are antecedent and consequent parts of one continuous line. To reinforce the symmetry: the typical Baroque dance was in two equal parts, each repeated.

The dialogues are also in two parts: 1–5 and 6–10. There is a seamless path from each dialogue to the next: one character from each overlaps to the next dialogue, with the exception of 9 and 10, with no overlaps from 8. Between 5 and 6 there is a dramatic break, with no overlap between. This is the dramatic mid-point, and we move from narrative background to the action. This, then, is the consequent to the antecedent history of 1–5.

This dramatic moment is highlighted by the music not of Bach, but of Bruckner. Instead of the quiet serenity that Bach's music presents (with a notable difference in 5, when Henrik plays a dynamic organ work by Bach), we hear music that is rhythmically accented, loud, massive. Something in the drama is about to change. This change is finally accomplished in 9 and 10, which provide the answer to a puzzling secret that is ever present.

There are four characters in this film: Johan, a wealthy man, who is head of the family, remote and angry; Marianne, Johan's former wife, who is friendly, interested but also remote; Henrik, Johan's son, who is an intensely feeling musician, beaten by life, neurotic bordering on psychotic; and Karen, Henrik's daughter, who is on the verge of blossoming and yet the victim of complexes that surround her. Another 'character' is Anna: Henrik's dead wife – Karin's mother – Johan's daughter-in-law.

While the four characters alternate dialogues, only one is in all of them: Anna. She is spoken about or her picture is present in every exchange. In 4, Henrik and Johan express their profound hatred for each other. When Henrik questions Johan about what he did to deserve such feelings from his father, Johan responds with an account of some event that happened more than 30 years ago, of somewhat minor importance. In 9, after Henrik's attempted suicide after Karin has left him, Johan confesses to Marianne that he was jealous of Henrik; he, too, was in love with Anna.

Anna's absence, and her meaning to those left behind, motivates most of the film. (In *Persona*, abandonment by the mother was an issue worked in somewhat different detail from that in *Saraband*. In the former, the lost child emerges as the artist from his journey of individuation with his anima on its way to being integrated; in the latter, the lost child is about to begin her journey of individuation.) Marianne, until the film's conclusion, is mainly narrator and the one assuming the pain (transference) of Johan, Henrik and Karin. The latter three have been profoundly affected by Anna's death two years earlier. Karin bears the burden of an atmosphere without feminine energy, and reaches out to Marianne to fill the void. Her father is in complete control of her: her provider, her teacher, probably her lover. The opportunity to begin her journey of individuation is thwarted by her father – by his dependence upon her, and her grandfather, by his anger towards Henrik.

In 8, the issue is brought to a violent conclusion when Karin confronts Henrik with a letter that Anna had written to him just before her death. Anna had expressed her fear of Henrik binding Karin to him too closely, too much, with the unspoken probability of a violation of boundaries; as she says in the film, 'Release her' and 'Don't take advantage of her in your role as teacher.' Anna's fears were justified. They were predictions of what was to occur. This dialogue concludes with Karin playing the *Saraband*, a dramatic moment when the piece heard entirely as background emerges into the foreground; Karin plays while Henrik is distraught. Bergman has brought the central musical moment into the foreground.

Karin was caught between a controlling father and a wretched grandfather. She chose neither, taking her first step towards writing her own life narrative. As a result, Henrik attempts – perhaps succeeding – suicide; Johan has a psychotic break, bemoans Anna's absence and seeks comfort from Marianne.

The remaining issue is that of the prologue/epilogue. In both, Marianne is sitting at a table that is laden with photographs – a reminder of Bergman's medium of choice. The prologue gives some narrative history, but in the epilogue Marianne becomes wistful, and speculative.

Her relationship with Johan had gradually faded away. She displays the photo of Anna that had appeared throughout the film. She says she often thinks about Anna, about 'Anna's feelings, Anna's love'. Finally, her thoughts drift towards her daughter, Martha, whom she seldom sees. Martha has been in a mental institution for many years.

At the film's conclusion, Marianne walks into Martha's room, sits directly in front of her, removes Martha's glasses and touches her face – for the first time.

The mother touches the child. *Persona* is completed.

References

1 Durrell, L. *Balthazar*. New York: Dutton, 1958, p. 183.
2 Durrell, L. *Clea*. New York: Dutton. 1960, p. 11.
3 Romanyshyn, R. *The Wounded Researcher: Research with Soul in Mind*. New Orleans, LA: Spring, 2007.
4 Eliot, T.S. 'East Coker'. *Four Quartets*. New York: Harcourt Brace & Company, p. 31.
5 Cater, N. *Electra*. New Orleans, LA: Spring, 2003, pp. 31–32.
6 Steene, B. 'Bergman's *Persona* through a native landscape'. In E. Michels (ed.), *Ingmar Bergman's* Persona. Cambridge: Cambridge University Press, 2000, pp. 24–44.
7 Sontag, S. 'Bergman's *Persona*'. In Michels, pp. 62–85.
8 Orr, C. 'Scenes from the class struggle in Sweden: *Persona* as Brechtian melodrama'. In Michels, pp. 86–109.

9 McLuhan, M. *Understanding Media*. New York: McGraw-Hill, 1964.
10 Lacan, J. and Miller, J. (eds). *The Seminar of Jacques Lacan*, Book VII. New York: Norton, 1992, p. 271.
11 Ibid.
12 Sophocles. *Electra*. H. Kitto, trans. Oxford: Oxford University Press, 1962, p. 124.
13 Rank, O. *The Double: A Psychoanalytic Study*. New York: New American Library, 1971.
14 Sontag, p. 73.
15 Jung, C. *Aion, Collected Works 9, II*, Para. 14.
16 Simon, J. 'The new leader'. In Michels, p. 173.
17 Michels, p. 17.
18 Jung, C. *Two Essays on Analytical Psychology, Collected Works* 7. Princeton, NJ: Princeton University Press, 1928, Para. 305.
19 Sharp, D. *C.G. Jung Lexicon*. Toronto: Inner City Books, pp. 98–99.
20 Reik, T. 'The three women in a man's life'. In P. Phillips (ed.), *Art and Psychoanalysis*. Cleveland, OH: Meridian, 1963, pp. 151–164.
21 Whitmont, E. *The Symbolic Quest*. Princeton, NJ: Princeton University Press, 1969, p. 156.
22 Sharp, p. 99.
23 Progoff, I. 'Waking dream and living myth'. In J. Campbell (ed.), *Myths, Dreams, and Religion*. Dallas, TX: Spring, 1970, p. 186.
24 Sharp, p. 14.
25 Jung, C. *The Archetypes and the Collective Unconscious, Collected Works 9, I*, Para. 498.

6

MUSIC AND ALCHEMY

Beethoven

Once again, we are confronted with a familiar conclusion: those who practise the creative arts think in and talk about them in ways very different from those who merely write and talk about the arts. Special consideration must be given to those who analyse the psyche and who deal with artists *per se*, for they dwell within the unconscious along with their analysands through the countertransference. At some level the artistic, non-language symbols that are different from ordinary language usage, as well as language-based novels and poetry, become shared in the powerful experience of psychoanalysis. The same cannot be said of the scientific community that attempts to deal with music through assumption based upon data.

> *'I don't think neuroscience can do more than confirm what talking to any composer would tell you.'*[1]

The quote by Sachs puts to shame much of what is written about music. This is not to negate Meyer's seminal thinking about experimental psychology, particularly gestalt, and its explanation of musical behaviour.[2] But his comments in that particular study were based upon a limited portion of the musical experience – and others have been stuck in much the same musical epoch. In short, they do not extend backwards to the Renaissance and beyond, or forward in time to the twentieth and twenty-first centuries, but remain in what we, in a manner of self-fulfilling prophecy, termed the 'common practice period': the music of Mozart, Haydn and Beethoven.

One of Langer's most perceptive discussions focuses on this point: that music imitates the living processes of breathing, tension and relaxation. Though the symbols used to communicate are different, these signifiers of life are common to both our living organism and the processed fulfilment of the intuitive creation of which I spoke in Chapter 1. Particularly where the music can be said to be 'organic', as in the Beethoven example discussed below, a discernible flow of energy – a living force – is experienced. (The visual manifestation of this idea is seen in the sculpture and architecture of Antonio Gaudi.) The problem was in deciding how to describe the musical factors that produce the analogues, thereby creating the feeling of life within the music.

Meyer solved that problem by means of a blending of music theory, information theory and gestalt psychology. Music operates within a system of expectation and fulfilment. The manner in which expectation is created is best described as a product of information theory. Emotion is created when expectation within the musical vocabulary is frustrated. Within a symbolic vocabulary of choice of pitches, subject to change as the musical epoch changes, 'rules' are established, precisely as they are established in language *per se*. There is a one-to-one relationship between the actual musical phenomena and the response to that phenomena which is evoked in the listener. A simple demonstration will illustrate this point.

At a piano, play the note C. Ask the question: 'What comes next?' This is admittedly an absurd question. However, the factual answer is that any of the 88 notes on the piano may come next. Now, choose C followed by D, and ask the same question. As you move up the C major scale, you realize that with each new note the choices become fewer, because a pattern is beginning to emerge; the greater the number of possibilities, the less the chance of correctly predicting what comes next. The pattern (C major scale) that gradually emerges is a cultural phenomenon, evolving from the late Renaissance, moving to the eighteenth and nineteenth centuries, and then moving away; music history, to this time, has been movement towards and away from harmony derived from these scales – tonality. The point is that, by the time you reach B, there is no question as to what comes next, and you can predict with 100 per cent reliability that it will be C, an octave higher than the C which began the process. This is the musical use of information theory of which Meyer spoke; stopping at B would cause frustration – the frustration of expectation in its lack of closure. It is this type of frustration and its eventual closure, handled with much greater sophistication, which propels music forward. Actual music is much more complicated, with a great variety of melodic, harmonic and rhythmic probabilities. But the basic concept is in the description of the unfolding of the C scale.

★

Before proceeding to a discussion of the energizing motif of Beethoven's *Symphony No. 5*, and the use of the term 'organic', it is necessary to consider the role of Jung's studies of alchemy:

> *The alchemical opus deals in the main not just with chemical experiments as such, but with something resembling psychic processes, expressed in pseudochemical language.*
>
> *. . . the gold he is seeking is not . . . the ordinary gold, it is the philosophical gold or even the marvelous stone . . . or the (ethereal stone), or finally the unimaginable hermaphroditic* rebis.[3]

Slowly, Jung moves through the transformative alchemical process to one where the final goal is not gold, but imagination. I will juxtapose examples from the opening of Beethoven's symphony with commentaries by von Franz and Edinger. First, I note the underlying musical assumptions; second, as each musical point is introduced, corresponding alchemical points will be added for comparison and collation. Gradually, a blended portrait emerges.

Musical discourse usually concentrates on separation and quantification. Separation involves extracting melody and/or harmony and/or rhythm, etc. from the total texture, rather than attaching quantification or some form of numerical measurements to the extracted materials. There are other variables: historical, sociological, acoustical, linguistic, biological – all of which become increasingly sophisticated additions to our understanding of music. Unfortunately, these processes of separation and quantification overlook the poetry of the music: the idea that music is what occurs between, rather than within, the notes.

Beethoven's *Symphony No. 5* is a work that yields little in the way of meaningful information about its melody (in this case, a mere motif), harmony or overall structure. This is either *not* a work like any other, or our vocabulary is so limited that we miss the total picture by concentrating on the details. This work is constructed of melodic/rhythmic motifs; but more important, it is constructed of pure energy, of forces that defy musical categorization. They are musical manifestations of physical gestures.

One of the most well-known musical motifs in the repertoire is the first four-note group of this work. In and of itself, it is of little interest; its power lies in the extensive use Beethoven makes of it throughout the symphony by means of imaginative transformations. It is the fundamental building block of the work, from which almost all else stems – described in terms useful in the arts, with a definite scientific tinge:

> *So in this image it is said that the angel bears the mystery of the basic material – of the cosmos we would say – and that is exactly what the alchemists, just like modern physicists, had in mind: that possibly all material phenomena went back to one basic material (prima seria).*[4]

Although Beethoven was probably not the first to use one theme or motif throughout an entire work, he was the first to do it so boldly. From his usage, the term 'organic' has emerged, meaning that there is a germinating idea from which the entire composition emerges:

> *Commenting upon alchemy's existence prior to epistemological criticism of the formation of images. 'This means one could fantasize at liberty, and describe, using the categories of one's own fantasy.'*[5]

The terms 'organic' and 'transmutation' are nearly synonymous. They are both about process, but from differing perspectives. While 'organic' looks at this music from a position of a single, small idea growing from the beginning of the work, 'transmutation' views the work as it is actually evolving from one use of the idea to another . . . always recognizable as the beginning idea. From the musical example, we see that the intervals change, not only in size but also direction. However, it is their rhythmic energy that is driving the piece; the mutations of the motif are always recognizable because they are presented in a similar rhythmic pattern.

The music starts with one line and a one-note accompaniment. As the line becomes inverted, the pace of events quickens, the texture thickens and there is a gathering of musical materials. The piece becomes louder and, seemingly, faster. This coagulation intensifies until it reaches a point of stasis. The process is then repeated . . . and repeated . . . and repeated . . . . Although the duration of the musical events varies, the process remains the same – unified simplicity leads to increasing complexity leads to stasis. The similarity between the imaginary flowchart and an example from a piece of a human's signal processed reading (voice analysis, heartbeats . . .) is remarkable. Music here appears very much a symbolic analogue of real living.

This music resembles the processes of human life in the metaphoric similarities of tension and relaxation, breathing, etc. The physical gesture of the rhythmic motif is then put through organic processes of growth and transformation in precisely the same way as was metal cooked by alchemists. And as from within the midst of the alchemical green fire the salamander emerges, so does Beethoven's 'fantasy of liberty' – individuation – emerge from the orchestral mixture.

★

One aspect of individuation that separates great artists from the less-than-greats is the expandable versus the finite container. Beethoven was perhaps the first composer who knew no boundaries. His quest was for immortality; he was the one who gave substance to the term 'genius'. His vision exceeded that of the known musical world, and he succeeded in casting his vision – or perhaps in mixing the elements – into the unknown, thereafter making it known. Bringing the unconscious into consciousness is a concept of equal importance to the creative arts as to depth psychology:

> *The great opposites of human nature in general, extraversion and introversion, play a tremendous role in the history of alchemy . . . when the two currents met, a strange switch occurred: the Greeks became interested in concrete material and the Egyptians in its psychological inner aspect. In spite of this development, the inner opposition and the play of their introverted and extraverted attitudes continued.*[6]

The opposites in Beethoven exist within the musical example used. His sketchbooks show the great care he took in articulating his musical designs, a very careful, intellectual process – that of an introvert. But the incredibly dynamic aspect of the actual, sounding music was powerfully extraverted. He lived his entire private life as a classic example of introversion, mainly because of his deafness; but he was also the extraverted man who shook his fist at God, and who withdrew the dedication of the *Eroica Symphony* from Napoleon.

The introvert who continually expands his inner horizon within the intellectual framework of his journey, is rare. In some, we can speak of a type of controlled passion: the last two words essentially in conflict with each other. And out of this conflict of opposites, the intellectual framework of the introvert and the controlled passion of the extravert, a mixing of elements termed 'opposites', a created artefact emerges. Beethoven passed this quality on to Mahler, and to Munch and Bergman. Freud passed it on to Jung; the latter's 'Confrontation with the Unconscious',[7] a dream that literally descends through the ages, illustrates an expansion of horizon similar to that of Beethoven.

There is a point at which Jung and Beethoven meet: that of the visionary. There were three distinct periods in Beethoven's creative career; *Symphony No. 5* was written during the middle period, as was the *Missa Solemnis* of which Aldous Huxley speaks so eloquently in the last quotation. During the last period, Beethoven produced works of astounding beauty and complexity; his creative world became totally divergent, even though he was totally deaf at the time. For Jung, his was a divergent world from the beginning. Neither of these men knew the meaning of boundaries.

Through our consideration of the tensions of opposites and alchemy, we can see how creative processes can be illuminated and clarified by alchemy. But this process of illumination cannot work in reverse: alchemy cannot be clarified by music. The symbol systems cannot be reversed. We can work musical materials, searching for analogies and metaphors, but we must always return to linear time (the experience of music as we hear it) and the language of Jung in order to communicate our insight to others.

From a different perspective:

> *Shakespeare shows us aspects of experience that doubtless existed before him, but he illuminates what we could not see without him.*[8]

It is precisely this quality of the unknown that must remain a mystery. We cannot know the non-language symbols used by creative artists; we can only experience them. But our feelings and intuition can speak of this experience. One never knows where the inner journey leads, and what findings along the way the creative artist and alchemist may choose to reveal. These two powerful currents of alchemical and creative processes are akin to two powerful rivers that run parallel, products of the same source. They move towards their destinations together; they will return, and recreate.

Aldous Huxley, on Beethoven:

> *Only music, and only Beethoven's music, and only this particular piece of Beethoven [Missa Solemnis] can tell us with any precision what Beethoven's conception of the blessedness at the heart of things actually was. If we want to know, we must listen – on a still June night, by preference, with the breathing of the invisible sea for background to the music and the scent of lime trees drifting through the darkness, like some exquisite soft harmony apprehended by another sense.*[9]

References

1 Sachs, O. 'When music heals'. *Parade Magazine*, 31 March 2002, p. 4.
2 Meyer, L. *Emotion and Meaning in Music*. Chicago and London: University of Chicago Press, 1956.
3 Jung, C. *Psychology and Alchemy, Collected Works 12*, Paras. 342–343.
4 Franz, M. von. *Alchemy: An Introduction to the Symbolism and the Psychology*. Toronto: Inner City Books, 1980, p. 66.
5 Edinger, E. *The Mysterium Lectures: A Journey through C.G. Jung's* Mysterium Coniunctionis. In J. Blackmer (ed.), Toronto: Inner City Books, 1995, p. 19.
6 Franz, M. von. *Alchemical Active Imagination*. Boston, MA: Shambhala, 1997, p. 16.
7 Jung, C. 'Confrontation with the unconscious'. In E. Jaffee (ed.), *Memories, Dreams, Reflections*. New York: Vintage, 1961, pp. 170–200.
8 Bloom, H. 'Preface'. In H. Corbin, *Alone with the Alone: Creative Imagination in the Sufism of Ibn 'Arabi*. Princeton, NJ: Princeton University Press, 1969, p. xv.
9 Huxley, A. *On Art and Artists*. New York: Meridian, 1962, p. 317.

7

GALLERY OF THE SOUL

Kahlo, Rivera, Munch

Responding to the questions raised by Fitzgerald's use of the word 'faith', and Bergman's appearance at the conclusion of *Persona* created pathways to understanding some of the unconscious motifs present in these works. Pater's comment that 'all art constantly aspires towards the condition of music'[1] is becoming increasingly clear, but much remains to be explored.

> *For the painter, sculptor and composer, the process brings foreground and background elements in a visual or auditory image or experience into the same spatial plane, superimposed or fused with one another. This leads to integrations and unification of visual and musical patterns, respectively.*[2]

I note that Rothenberg places both music and visual art 'into' rather than onto the 'same spatial plane'. He envisions arts fused in experience. But, how can that be so? Music is said to exist in time, while visual art exists in space. There is an element of reality in the characterization, but it is based upon the work of art being an object, rather than a process. Let us consider this idea, utilizing the formulation of the creative process discussed earlier: the journey from X to artefact.

There is a Frida Kahlo oil on cardboard titled 'Diego and me', which depicts the blended faces of Frida and Diego Rivera. It is precisely the image that Bergman used in *Persona*. In the Kahlo, it is a symbol of the blending of two separate lives into one, a desire of Frida's not shared by Diego. Two heads in the space of one: the emotion of the blending, *per se*, overwhelms the unreality. One head is not made of two separate beings, except in the unconscious.[3]

Theirs was a relationship of two creative artists, whose marriage was simultaneously loving and dysfunctional. Their respective biographies illustrate love for each other and the utmost respect for each other's art: Diego on Frida: 'She is a better painter than I am.'[4] At one point, he described their marriage as non-competitive, but tumultuous. And Frida, who was initially a young painter seeking the advice of Mexico's most famous artist – who became his lover, then his wife – was a lifetime admirer and supporter of Diego's art and politics. The intricacies of their relationship, as experienced in their art, yield valuable insights regarding the complexities of these two monumental talents. Both of their unconscious psyches brought them directly into the archetypes, but the archetypes themselves differed markedly.

> *Art is the appeal to the instinct of the common in men* [Ellie Faure told Diego Rivera]. *We recognize one another by the echoes it awakens in us.*[5]

> *The only thing I know is that I paint because I need to, and I paint always whatever passes through my head, without any other consideration.*[6]

Two quotes from Virginia Woolf's biographer add insight to these two from the biographies of Rivera and Kahlo:

> *She envies the painters . . . able to penetrate through . . . portraits to the complexity and intrigue of character.*[7]

> *Her* [VW's] *illness became her language.*[8]

This last quote is included as a bridge between Kahlo and Woolf – from words to painting. Frida's illness was physical; she suffered a traumatic injury at the age of 19, which left her in pain throughout her life. Crippled and subjected to dozens of surgical attempts to heal her, and unable to have children, she began to paint while recuperating from this traumatic event. She was always an individualist: perhaps alienated from society, perhaps burdened by her inquisitive nature and intelligence, perhaps manifesting the soul of the creative artist accessing her unconscious. Frida developed a 'language' that was beyond personal. One sees through her skin, through her heart, to the very essence of her being . . . and through her into the collective.

We discover emotions that move directly from Kahlo's paintbrushes into our own deepest sense of being – X completed. We witness her vulnerability and loneliness in *The Flying Bed*, her horror of personal violence done to others and emotional violence done to her by Rivera, symbolically, in *A Few Little Pricks*, the existential futility of the *Suicide of Dorothy Hale* and her physical pain in *The Broken Column* and *The Wounded Deer*. We also find her reaching out in formats larger than the personal, such as *Moses*, a commentary of Freud's *Moses and Monotheism*, and in *What the Water Gave Me*, reminiscent of one of the movements of Mahler's *Symphony No. 3*.

Her main focus was her self-portraits. In these, we see her reflcetions on the two tragedies of her life – her accident and Diego[9] – brought to life. There is a constant change and renewal in her dress and background of these portraits, but the face remains the same. Often, there is a vision of Rivera somewhere, even implanted in her forehead. The best description of this relationship, as seen in these portraits with Rivera's presence so pronounced, and of their life together in general, was enmeshment. Her artistic language became the compensatory communication of her physical and emotional difficulties.

Kahlo paints the personal: what 'passes through my head'. Rivera paints the social: 'the instinct of the common man'. Rivera as a creative artist painted portraits, as did Kahlo. And Kahlo, who deeply shared Rivera's politics, painted social themes. Her evolution as an artist began, and ended, with her own pain – physical and emotional. Her pathway to and from her unconscious was unmediated by social forces, as was Rivera's. Hers was a personal agony, while his was a deeply felt social awareness. While there was a powerful commitment to her on his part, it did not include an awareness of the constant pain his infidelities caused her, particularly when one of his affairs was with her sister. Personal anguish is not often present in Rivera's subjects; the anguish is from the subject. But with Kahlo, it is the emotional and physical condition of the subject that presents the anguish.

Kahlo transmitted her private despair, whereas Rivera's focused on the national despair of Mexico. He concentrated her imagery on the magic central to Mexican culture; he focused on Mexican myth. Both found a literary voice in Latin American magic realism. Whereas Kahlo's evolution was inner directed, Rivera's was typical of the experimentalists of his era.

Impressionist and Cubist periods preceded his creation of and concentration on Mexican nationalism. His murals were not for the private viewing necessitated by the size of Kahlo's paintings, but were massive narratives on the inner and outer walls of buildings. Masses of people could view Rivera's work, simultaneously, and its political messages helped stir the country's latent nationalistic pride. It was as if the personal sufferings of Kahlo's work were magnified to a zeitgeist. Suffering is the common state of existence here; the personal and collective, because of the unitary and intermingled psyches, present two different but related archetypes. (This forms part of the discussion of Chapter 9.)

★

In Edvard Munch, we find a blending of personal (*The Scream*) and societal suffering (*Anxiety*):

> *In my art I have tried to explain myself, life and its meaning. I have also meant to help others to clarify their lives.*[10]

The *Evening on Karl Johan* is an extension of *Anxiety*. Here, Munch blends the foreground of *Anxiety* with the background of *The Scream*. Solitary figure and crowd are interchangeable. This is a similar concept to the Kahlo/Rivera portrait versus mural distinction. It also demonstrates the several meanings of suffering: personal and societal, each of which has further extensions.

Here, we are discussing both the personal and societal aspects of suffering. Each meaning of the term has further extensions; for example, isolation and alienation are present in both Munch and Van Gogh. Suffering is an existential state of being; it affects all human beings. Some artists have the ability to bring it into consciousness. It must be powerful to be experienced, and it is through our attempts to resist and/or overcome it that we become aware of its presence. Some artists choose to confront their own suffering by forcibly acknowledging its presence – by presenting it publicly through some artistic medium. It is, then, confessional, a reading of one's own unconscious psyche for the illumination of others.

In his book *Memories, Dreams, Reflections*, Jung describes a dream in which he explores a house he did not know, even though he described it as 'my house'.[11] He investigates the various rooms, afterward realizing that he must descend a series of staircases to further understand where he is. On arriving at the lowest level, he awoke; he had ended this journey. This was the origin of the collective unconscious, the domain of the archetypes.

I have maintained that the goal of the arts is to bring the unconscious into consciousness. In this chapter, I note two conceptions of suffering. The implication is that personal suffering is the rhizome from which societal suffering grows. The personal pain of Kahlo moves from her into the soil, and back to her, again; it is self-nurturing. The societal pain of Rivera moves from him into the soil, but upon its return spreads out to be absorbed by many.

The metaphor being used is limited . . . and limiting. Jung descends the staircases, and most would say that the unconscious resides somewhere in the depths of the body, for the descent is downward, moving internally. It is there, grounded; it rises up when summoned by the unconscious. It not only appears to descend, but it does so in a uni-linear direction . . . that is, downward and into the body's midst.

However, based upon the differentiations in 'suffering', and the variations in other artistic threads that bind these chapters' discussions to each other, I conclude that unconscious is not a flat point of arrival, an undifferentiated surface. Rather, it is a series of multidirectional, interwoven threads. Points of contact among these threads are, while illusive, also transferable within this container called the unconscious. The conclusion of the voyage through the unconscious is, of course, the archetypes.

The murals of Rivera and the portraits of Kahlo present to us the archetypes of human suffering. While the overarching point of arrival is suffering, Kahlo and Rivera present one final step prior to reaching the archetype. Each must undergo one final layer of decoding, a last step through the mythical and social symbolism being used. In the case of Munch's *Frieze of Life*, this step is not necessary. The answer that Jung found at the bottom level of his house, the two skulls symbolizing the key to the collective unconscious, are present in the immediacy of Munch's paintings.

★

Munch's drypoint *The Woman* (1895) depicts a woman of spring, a whore and sorrow. This same group occurs, with slight variations, in a lithograph of *The Woman* (1899).[12] This trio of stages is the life cycle of woman. The idea is also present, with specifically psychological descriptions, in Reik's analysis of Offenbach's opera *The Tales of Hoffmann*. Of the three female characters, he writes:

> *Here are three women in one, or one woman in three shapes: the one who gives birth, the one who gives sexual gratification, the one who brings death. Here are the three aspects woman has in a man's life: the mother, the mistress, the annihilator. The first and last characters meet in the middle.*[13]

Compression of archetypal motifs, which we see in the painters, and in Reik's analysis of the opera, occur in many forms; we will discuss two of them in the final chapters: the *Alexandria Quartet*, and Mahler's grand cycle of symphonies in the concluding chapter.

One of the most powerful depictions of spiritual journeys in the arts is Munch's *Frieze of Life* – a poem of life, love and death. Attracted to these subjects because of their proximity to Munch's personal experiences, the universality found in them activated his unconscious psyche:

> *I do not believe in art that does not spring from man's yearning to open up his heart. All art, literature as well as music, must come from the heart: art is the distillation of man's very life blood.*[14]

These words could have been written by Mahler, Bergman and others; they restate the quote above (note 10) by Munch himself.

Love occupies a significant position in the Frieze. *Attraction* shows the man wrapped in a woman's hair, in several different settings; *The Kiss* is similar in its variety of media and construction:

> *The trees and the air and all the earth vanished and I looked into a new world I never before had known.*[15]

In *Encounter in Space* the lovers meet, and in *The Flower of Love* we see them engulfed within the petals of the flower:

> *Only few meet in the one tremendous flame – where they both can be completely one.*[16]

Unlike the stark sexual symbolism of O'Keeffe's flowers, Munch portrays the power of romantic love, a more conservative universe. Both are powerful, and both engage the viewer in a time-orientated period of contemplation. But there is a difference in the two: Munch's attention seems directed inward from the painting to an absorbing unconscious; O'Keeffe's seems projected from the unconscious to the painting. There is a distinct difference in the cultural values of sexuality from the Romanticism/Victorianism of Munch's era to that of O'Keeffe's feminism.

However, there exists a personal conflict in Munch's depictions of the Romanticism of love as the lovers in *The Kiss*, *Encounter in Space* and *The Flower of Love* break apart in another phase of the Frieze.

In Munch's life, love was ephemeral. It gave way to *Vampire* and *Jealousy*. In *Vampire*, as in the scene from *Persona* where the two women assume the exact position of Munch's painting, the woman's hair falls over the man who is pressing himself into her lap. If we take Munch's title literally, she is sucking life's blood out of him. The idealized woman who was *Madonna*, 'the woman who gives herself away – and obtains a Madonna's painful beauty'[17] has evolved into the woman at the conclusion of this episode of Romantic love:

> *He buried his face in her lap and felt two burning lips in the back of his neck – it gave him a freezing sensation through his body – of freezing lust.*[18]

Love has turned to *Ashes*:

> *There was something in her expression that made him feel fearful – he did not know what it was.*[19]

The lovers have separated, and he is left in the isolation and abbreviation of *Jealousy*.

We now see why the central characters of *Woman in Three Stages* have returned: the poem of life, love and death is an autobiography of Edvard Munch. The suffering that evolved in his paintings is a part of the human condition that is most difficult to communicate since it reaches so deeply into the artist's profoundly personal unconscious that it communicates several archetypes simultaneously: love and death. A consideration of most of his titles of the individual works in the Frieze shows that even the subgroups within love and death are archetypes; for example, *Puberty*, *Madonna*, *Jealousy* . . . and the entire sickness motif.

We see a group of people coming towards us:

> *Everything became so empty and he felt so alone . . . People who passed by looked so strange and awkward and he felt as if they looked him stared at him all these faces pale in the evening light.*[20]

In the important transitional group, Munch is seen as separated from the group. This same crowd is seen in *Anxiety*, with the sea in the background; a solitary man in *Despair*, on a bridge, again with the sea as backdrop. All comes to full frontal force in *The Scream*: 'A great scream went through nature.'[21] The human beings of the previous paintings have turned into a living skeleton, life on its path to death, a powerfully resisting force shattering the universe . . . an epiphany unlike any other in the world of art.

Death is the remaining archetype. The voiceless terror on the face of the little girl in *Dead Mother and Child*, succeeding *The Sick Child* and *Death in the Sickroom* brings us nearly to the completion of Munch's narrative. He was profoundly affected by the deaths he experienced as a child, particularly those of one of his sisters and his mother. Tragedy at such a vulnerable age must have forced powerful feelings inward, and condensation into the unconscious. This is akin to Mahler's experience of his younger brother's death, which was to haunt him throughout his life and lead to many powerful compositions, as well as a general attraction to themes of death and resurrection.

The death motif also influenced Kahlo: not death, *per se*, but perhaps dying – the consequences of a catastrophic accident and a lifetime of pain. The numerous examples of childhood trauma in the lives of creative artists lead to an interesting conjecture: the creative person who compensates for early disaster by healing themself, and projecting onto others their efforts so that they, too, may heal. (Munch says something similar in note 10, above.)

But Munch does not conclude with death. The final comment on the process, completed after the death sequence but before the cycle of love paintings – and not part of the Frieze, is *Fertility*. A buried skeleton provides the rhizome from which a tree has sprouted. On either side of the tree, a naked man and woman are gazing at each other. Love that had evolved from death provides a resurrection. 'Art is the distillation of man's very life blood' (see note 14).

In relation to the idea of putting his paintings together in groupings rather than having them separated, Munch stated:

> *When they were placed together, a sound went through them right away, and they became quite different than when they were separate. They became a symphony.*[22]

★

There are many references to music in the arts. What is particularly meaningful is the blending of media into one experience: the time of music with the space of art. The musical score, especially since the 1950s, is often a visual work of art, but this score is merely a set of performance instructions. The music is a sounding, temporal phenomenon. This reality cycles back to the subject of time. In the case of this usually complex music, it is the time spent in unravelling the complexities – just as it is the time spent gazing at a painting – that is the critical feature. It is the absorbing, decoding, searching for X that we are addressing, what Langer refers to as contemplation:

> *we see that in all the plastic arts there is a 'time of contemplation' filled with successive psychic facts, more or less prolonged, and of which the aesthetic content is important.*[23]

Many painters, particularly Klee, have commented upon the time of painting. It is assumed, but as a pathway to the unconscious it needs further explanation. An article in the *New York Times* reviews an exhibit of Gauguin: 'Maker of Myth':

> *Storytelling is the show's main theme, the specific idea being that Gauguin's use of narrative set him apart from modernist contemporaries like the Impressionists.*[24]

The writer, Holland Carter, utilizes the terms 'storytelling' and 'narrative'. Clearly, these terms of verbal communication are viable in depictions of paintings. He continues:

> *While they* [Impressionists] *were stripping their art of symbolic and personal content to move forward to abstraction, Gauguin was piling exactly these elements on and looking backward to old-fashioned things like historical painting, religious art, and myth.*[25]

'Myth?' Like the paintings of Kahlo and Rivera, Gauguin is touching the archetypes. (And 'backwards to old-fashioned things' is reminiscent of the Romanticism of *Tender is the Night* and, as we shall soon see, *To the Lighthouse*.)

In that large room extending the Gallery of the Soul, the room that symbolizes the depth of the unconscious, painters, novelists, composers and filmmakers are exploring that which is there to become known – their own unconscious psyches – that we are continuing to illuminate.

Virginia Woolf comments upon painters being able to penetrate portraits, becoming great biographers . . . 'to the very complexity or intrigue of character'.[26] In *To the Lighthouse*, Woolf created just such a biographer – Lily Briscoe.

References

1 Pater, W. *The Renaissance*. Mineola, NY: Dover, 2005, p. 90.
2 Rothenberg, A. *Creativity and Madness*. Baltimore, NY: Johns Hopkins University Press, 1994, p. 28.
3 Ketterman, A. 'Diego and I'. *Frida Kahlo 1907–1954*. London: Taschen, 2009, p. 79.
4 Herrera, H. *Frida: A Biography of Frida Kahlo*. New York: Harper & Row, 1983, p. 306.
5 Wolfe, B. *The Fabulous Life of Diego Rivera*. Chelsea, MI: Scarborough House, 1960, p. 109.
6 Herrera, p. 254.
7 Lee, H. *Virginia Woolf*. New York: Vintage, 1999, p. 12.
8 Ibid., p.172.
9 Herrera, H. p. 289.
10 Torjusen, B. *Words and Images of Edvard Munch*. Chelsea, VT: Chelsea Green, 1986, p. 141.
11 Jung, C. 'Confrontation with the unconscious'. In E. Jaffee (ed.), *Memories, Dreams, Reflections*. New York: Vintage, 1961, p. 159.
12 Torjusen, pp. 127–128.

13 Reik, T. 'The three women in a man's life'. In W. Phillips (ed.), *Art and Psychoanalysis.* Cleveland, OH: World Publishing, pp. 151–164.
14 Strang, R. *Edvard Munch.* G. Culverwell, trans. New York: Abbeyville, 1977, p. 31.
15 Torjusen, p. 85.
16 Ibid., p. 101.
17 Ibid., p. 92.
18 Ibid., p. 102
19 Ibid., p. 105.
20 Ibid., p. 131.
21 Ibid., p. 136.
22 Ibid., p. 142.
23 Sovrin, E. 'Time in the plastic arts'. In. S. Langer (ed.), *Reflections on Art.* New York: Oxford University Press, 1968, p. 123.
24 Carter, H. 'Gauguin: maker of myth'. *New York Times*, 25 February 2011, p. 19.
25 Ibid.
26 Lee, p. 12.

8

TO THE LIGHTHOUSE

It is now becoming increasingly clear that many of Jung's main concepts appear in works of art, and that these works of art validate the concepts. This chapter illuminates several of these concepts, simultaneously. It is notable that, within this large room at the end of the Gallery, threads appear to be ever-thickening, interweaving as it were. Some intersect ideas already presented in this book, while still others present new combinations amidst a plethora of possibilities – the very nature of symbolic languages.

★

Virginia Woolf comments upon painters' ability to 'penetrate portraits', becoming great biographers 'to the complexity or intrigue of characters'.[1] She encapsulates this idea in the figure of the painter Lily Briscoe in her novel *To the Lighthouse* (1927).

This novel orbits around the figure of Mrs Ramsay in two simultaneous realities: the relationship between her and her husband, Ramsay, and the effect of this relationship on those around them, and her particular relationship to Lily.[2] In the last section of the book, 'The Lighthouse', Lily emerges as the central character, revealing an archetypal meaning of the novel. All threads coalesce around the final stroke of her paintbrush . . . all meaning . . . the unconscious fully engaged.

'The Lighthouse' concludes the novel with the simultaneous realities of Ramsay's voyage to the lighthouse and the creation of Lily's painting of St Ives, the Ramsays' vacation home. This latter reality is the structural foundation of the chapter – the summation of the entire novel's psychological explorations. The painting was left unfinished ten years ago, and Lily is attempting to recapture the life of that previous visit. This section is one of the finest descriptions of the creative process in literature. We are witnesses to Lily's journey from superficial landscape, as in her previous paintings, to a profound realization of the subject – the house – as an assembly of psyches. These psyches are mainly treated as extensions of Mrs Ramsay. This is what Lily is attempting to understand, as she repeatedly steps back from her easel; the perspective she increasingly gains is not that of space, but of the various personae of the novel, in time.

Perspective in the linear sense would apply to Rivera's use of spatial separation to delineate space and/or time, or Munch's use in order to rapidly force attention onto the terrifying face of *The Scream*. However, this perspective is akin to the portraiture of Kahlo that Woolf noted in the quote above: the 'complexity and intrigue' of the house at St Ives. It is the discovery of the perspective of Lily herself in the environment that leads directly to her individuation.

The various people who are at St Ives during their summer vacation are ultimately backdrops to the Ramsays.

Aside from Lily, particular interest focuses on the two youngest children, James and Cam. At the novel's beginning, Mrs Ramsay is sitting by the window, looking out into the garden and reading a fairy tale to James.

An argument without resolution between Mr and Mrs Ramsay interrupts the reading. All of the people in the narrative will have to deal with this behaviour between them. With these two lines of dialogue, the pathway of the novel has been given. It begins with an understanding of the relationship between the Ramsays, which is condensed in the fairy tale that is being read to James: *The Fisherman and His Wife*.[3] Summary: one day the fisherman catches a flounder. The flounder is, in fact, an enchanted prince. Since the fish is capable of speaking, the fisherman returns it to the water, trailing blood. Upon returning home, the fisherman's wife berates him for not asking something of the flounder as a reward for returning it to the water. She complains that they live in a pig-sty and wants a nicer home. Against his will, the fisherman returns to the sea and makes his request for a nicer home; it is immediately granted.

His wife is still not satisfied, and makes increasingly more extravagant demands upon her husband to deliver to the flounder. Although it becomes increasingly difficult for the fisherman to obey his wife, he does – and each wish is immediately fulfilled.

The movement is from pig-sty to nice hut, cottage, castle where the wife is queen, a palace where she is empress, to a city for an empress where she is pope. Finally, still dissatisfied, she demands to be 'even as God'. Immediately granted, they return – to their pig-sty.

Fairy tales explore the unconscious psyche. Profound exploration moves beyond the personal into the collective.

A creative artist such as Woolf deliberately chose this particular fairy tale to inform the reader of what was to occur. But Woolf coded her message to necessitate a reader's participation that would lead to the unconscious. In Beethoven's *Symphony No. 5*, subtlety was not a concern; in *To the Lighthouse*, participation by the reader in decoding the novel was of paramount importance. In the use of the fairy tale, Woolf provided the key.

The Fisherman and His Wife is a story of psychological violence in the behaviours of the two persons involved: one active, the other passive. It differs from physical violence in that there are no exchanges that involve wounding caused by physical action. The passive fisherman and his aggressive wife each feed upon the behaviours and needs of the other; they each need to feel necessary. This need for fulfilling a part of the other assures that this co-dependency will continue, with each filling a negative space in the other. It is this catering to negativity that perpetuates a dysfunctional relationship. In order to retain their unacknowledged hostility to each other, they must continually repeat those actions that provoke it – projections that have both masochistic and sadistic properties. It is not a way of fulfilling life positively; it is, in fact, a deeply psychological piercing of the psyche.

Beyond this summary lies the journey into the unconscious, thoughts that can be used as a template to ultimately fashion the figures of Mr and Mrs Ramsay, finally arriving at Lily's triumphant utterance at the novel's conclusion: 'It was done, it was finished . . . I have had my vision.'

The fisherman and his wife speak to each other: the same command and response is repeated seven times. (It is not a coincidence that the exchange regarding the trip to the lighthouse is repeated seven times.) The wife commands the fisherman to 'Do it!' and the fisherman does as commanded, but is increasingly uncomfortable, then apprehensive regarding the consequences of his trips to the flounder. As the wife's commands become increasingly grandiose, the fisherman's responses mimic those of nature or consciousness: upset, nearing neurosis. The weather and the sea (the unconscious brought to consciousness) begin to threaten; the colours of the sky and water move from clear blue to murky and roiling black. The fisherman eventually reaches a form of psychotic break.

The flounder, the fish which in some ways is a Christ figure, is the only giving character in the group. After trailing blood when being returned to the sea, he constantly re-emerges to do good deeds for the fisherman. His journey lies between the unconsciousness of the sea and the consciousness of his dealings with the fisherman, and attempts to placate the extraordinary insecurity of the wife. But she cannot be satisfied. Her journey remains unfulfilled, as does that of the fisherman. There is no heroic return for either of them. They return to their point of origin with no bounty, no knowledge to share, no potential for growth. They are in stasis.

From the opening of *To the Lighthouse*, 'Yes, if it's fine tomorrow', followed by 'But, it won't be fine', we are aware of an undercurrent that in the later sections of the novel increases to psychological violence. The opening exchange is continued in the next few parts of 'The Window', the novel's first section, and is the catalyst for the reality of Mr Ramsay's voyage to the lighthouse in the third section. The fairy tale is a microcosm of the main conflict of the novel, a conflict that ultimately engulfs everyone.

★

Lily Briscoe stands in front of her painting of the house in St Ives. This house is the family structure in which the conflicts between the Ramsays were acted out. The house is, in its deteriorating condition, the Ramsays.

Mr Ramsay rejects the first calling to the lighthouse, in 'The Window'; he accepts the calling in *The Lighthouse*. 'Refusal of the call converts the adventure into a negative.'[4] As with the fisherman, acting against his own self-interest can be destructive, not only personally but to those around one.[5] Ramsay pauses at the threshold just as the fisherman did each time he sought the flounder. But he never crossed it, afraid of the consequences of dealing with his wife. Ramsay avoids the lighthouse, and its masculinity, for many years.

Although Ramsay's life was devoted to teaching and the writing of books, Mrs Ramsay had no notion of what his work meant.[6] This became clear with a direct question to their son Andrew. She could not even understand his answer.[7] Ramsay was faced with a woman who was described as formidable; he often wondered what was behind her beauty and splendour. This insecurity in his relationship also turns upon himself; when he cannot solve a meaningless intellectual problem, he assumes himself a failure who will always be unable to reach the intellectual adulation he feels he deserves.[8] This is further enforced when he has an important visiting lecture cancelled.

Ramsay's insecurities are manifested by a sense of alienation and isolation, and his fear of 'perishing'; he is constantly muttering phrases from Cowper's *The Castaway*. These insecurities are compensated for by his combination of blustering and bullying behaviours. Children and guests protect themselves by remaining aloof; his youngest children, Cam and James, develop a hatred for him. Lily's feelings alternate among admiration bordering on love, semi-fear, concern for his well-being and a hint at need of a father image.

Mrs Ramsay has reached a working accommodation with him, her second choice in her love life. Depending upon how her feelings were projected, seemingly through tolerant disinterest in her husband, it is likely that Mr Ramsay would intuit that his wife would consider him, as in Molly Bloom's soliloquy, the same as any other man.[9] It could not have been pleasant being Mr Ramsay. He was at times pitifully dependent, needing sympathy, and at other times completely self-involved, ignoring his student, Tansley, or bitingly aggressive as with James, his wife's favourite child.

Woolf describes Ramsay as he finally journeys to the lighthouse. He is in his boat, heading for the lighthouse; he has just caught a fish, which lies in the bottom of the boat . . . all the while muttering poetry.[10] Shortly thereafter, he finally acknowledges James with his first compliment in his son's memory.[11] Something has shifted; perhaps it is the re-utterance of the 'perished' motif from Cowper's poem, now emerging from the blue of the imagination to the green of reality: Mrs Ramsay is dead.

Ramsay the fisherman. Passive. Victimized by his own inactions. And Mrs Ramsay/Virginia Woolf: true victim of the patriarchal residue of Victorianism. How well they fit – how completely they needed each other.

★

Mrs Ramsay, the fisherman's wife, organizes life at St Ives, while the other participants in this drama of psychological violence float on and off stage. Ramsay, one of the main participants, excludes himself from all things that do not pertain to him. It is left to Mrs Ramsay to be in charge, which perfectly fits her character.

The choice of the fairy tale was deliberate; the fisherman and his wife are sharply drawn, as are the concepts of depth psychology drawn from them. In *Who's Afraid of Virginia Woolf?*,[12] Edward Albee distils the psychological violence derived from the fairy tale and, transferred to St Ives, it became a powerfully activated drama. Virginia Woolf herself viewed Mr and Mrs Ramsay, particularly the latter, in a far more subtle, and complex, fashion. But it is not difficult to understand Albee's distillation of the Ramsays, particularly the wife.

In her discussion of the fairy tale *Old Rindkrank*, von Franz notes:

> *Since the masculine element is so vague, and the princess-daughter is more fully characterized – her fate being central – we know that this is probably a story about the animus . . .*[13]

Jung's concept of the 'inner masculine side of a woman' is as follows:[14]

> *The great problem of the animus is that when a woman is un-conscious of her animus, it links up with her emotional side and she becomes the proverbial 'bull in a china shop'.*[15]

These lines regarding the animus transfer from the fisherman's wife to Mrs Ramsay. Also relevant is Cater's description of the mother archetype as 'psychopathology as seen in the controlling mother or the suffering martyr'.[16] One such point in the Ramsays' relationship is where her response to his marriage proposal is answered affirmatively. She repeats her 'yes' to him several times.[17]

In *Ulysses*, the atmosphere for Joyce's pastoral setting – Molly's soliloquy and the novel's conclusion – utilizes her repetitive 'yes' to a conclusion of thundering power.[18] In Pater's terms, it is *musically* illuminated in Stephen Albert's *Flower of the Mountain*, a work of emotion equivalent to the best of Mahler.

Correlations between *To the Lighthouse* and Joyce's *Ulysses* are remarkable. *Ulysses* occurs in one day, as do 'The Window' and 'The Lighthouse' sections of Woolf's novel. Joyce's stream of consciousness is somewhat softened in Woolf's usage; in the latter, linguistic constructions and oblique references do not require a key for understanding.

The first and last sentences of Woolf's novel begin with the word 'Yes', and 'Yes' is the concluding word in Joyce's.

Molly Bloom is passionate, animated, present, while Mrs Ramsay is cool, remote.[19] Her acceptance of Mr Ramsay's marriage proposal is lukewarm, a giving-in . . . he's as good as another . . . while the animated Molly reflects with passion but also a mere hint of the dismissive attitude of Mrs Ramsay; passion, however, wins out.[20]

Both women are in character in these quotes. Molly has been suspect for her 'Spanish ways' throughout the novel; she is passion to Leopold's passivity. This is another point of transference between the novels referencing the fairy tale: male and female roles reversed. While both women accept and apparently reject their men simultaneously, Molly's earthiness is in direct contrast to Mrs Ramsay's lack of affect. One could, perhaps, separate Romanticism from Victorianism with a stripe down the middle of a painting, as Lily does at the conclusion of *To the Lighthouse.*

Mrs Ramsay presents issues of increasing complexity. In 'The Lighthouse', the simultaneous realities of Lily's painting and Ramsay's voyage are the threads that are clearly the foci. Of these, Lily's painting, the unfolding act of creation, is more prominent. In 'The Window', Mrs Ramsay's narrative was the main thread; the life at St Ives was presented in a series of events and reactions, leading in some cases to overt responses but in others as psychological indicators of the general dysfunction of the household – including the visitors.

These indicators were presented in 'The Window' in a combination of symbolic disguise and stream of consciousness. The symbols blend into the stream unheard and seemingly unfelt . . . the literary equivalent of the musical leitmotif. To briefly cycle back to Pater's theory of all arts aspiring to the condition of music: Wagner used this technique of direct attention in his *Nibelung* cycle, whereas Beethoven allowed the opening motif of *Symphony No. 5* to emerge as part of an organic process. Britten in *Peter Grimes*[21] and Debussy in *Pelléas et Mélisande*[22] used series of motifs as orchestral commentary, while Mahler somehow managed to have a truly universal motif present, and evolving, throughout his symphonies, often without text.

(The middle section of *To the Lighthouse*, 'Time Passes', differs from the outer two in that it consists almost entirely of narrative, with some dialogue in brackets. This resembles the structure of *Tender is the Night*, in that both novels have contrasting middle sections that serve as information-producing breaks in the novels' progress. This can be heard most definitively in the powerful 'Sea Interludes' in *Peter Grimes*. I am not suggesting a deliberate literary approach to a musical technique, but on the most profound aesthetic level, that of contrast, the utilization of contrast in this manner is interesting.)

The leitmotifs of Mrs Ramsay, introduced in 'The Window' and fully developed in 'The Lighthouse', include her recurring unease over money to repair the shed, the ever-present depression manifested in her critical evaluations of others, her condescending and highhanded attitude towards Lily, and her obsessive need to dominate and control life at St Ives.

In one particular incident, Mrs Ramsay bemoans the fact that Cam and James are still awake hours after they have been put to bed. She comments that they are growing up too fast; she calms them, ignoring their fear of the symbol of death, a skull, hanging on the bedroom wall; she simultaneously blames the adults for provoking the incident. Everyone is at fault. She placates the children's fear of death by wrapping her shawl around the skull. She placates her own fear of growing old, and death, when, looking at her neck and shoulders in the mirror, she avoids her face;[23] another manifestation of her denial of reality, not covered up as in the children's fear of death, but avoided . . . mirror, mirror on the wall. But the clearest representations of Mrs Ramsay's psyche are in her conflicts with Ramsay. In these, we experience the fisherman's wife possessed by her own animus, seeking to become the masculine energy in the marriage.

From the controlling aspect of Mrs Ramsay's behaviour, its projections of a powerful animus, I seek a thread to lead further into her unconscious. Again, the fisherman's wife: a woman who must have everything she wants (which is never enough), who has a husband but no relationship with him other than commanding him to fulfil her needs, a woman to whom all objects in the outer world relate only to her.

There is a thread in the lack of feeling between the Ramsays. His inability to relate to her is born of insecurity and underdeveloped sense of self. The inability of Mrs Ramsay to have a real relationship with any other human being is an aspect of narcissism that occurs in the fisherman's wife; in both of them, the world exists as an extension of the Self. We do not have information about Mrs Ramsay's narrative, except that Ramsay was not her first choice of husband. We also know that her attempt at controlling her family and the visitors at St Ives was largely unsuccessful, with the exception of Lily who finally overcomes Mrs Ramsay's influence over her at the novel's conclusion, demonstrated by the artistic gesture that is Lily's entrance into individuation. We do know that Mrs Ramsay suffers the same fate as the Queen in *Snow White*: gazing in the mirror does not fulfil the narcissistic vision of her Self. Narcissism has cast her as the central focus; animus possession created a necessity for controlling everyone; animus projection was the method of control.

Mrs Ramsay failed at those things she wished to accomplish. She and her husband lived an existence filled with disappointment, in themselves and in each other. Their projections upon each other created a marriage that resembled an armed truce; all the characters felt the horrible tensions, and suffered accordingly. Only the Ramsays seemed unaware. She died young, and he finally attempted to heal the lack of communication with James, on their voyage to the lighthouse.

But ultimately, *To the Lighthouse* is a novel about Lily Briscoe. It is a powerful study of the emerging unconscious, through painting and through her understanding of the Ramsays. It is as if one could be holding the hand of Frida Kahlo as she worked upon one of her self-portraits, in contact with her inner world as she worked. But in Lily's case, it is the actual act of painting that is continually energizing and re-energizing her inner voyage of discovery – a journey that Kahlo had taken earlier in her life. Lily is approaching the moment when she is ready to receive X, to witness its calling. She is about to create a narrative, similar to music, in which words do not matter. Lily's epiphany does not lead to an artefact; it merely allows the creative act to begin. The work, now, will be Lily's.

Lily Briscoe's act of creating provides the novel with a crescendo typical of dramatic music – a dynamic gesture that was so much a part of music of the Romantic epoch. Woolf engulfs the reader in the emergence of Lily's unconscious.

There is a painting in search of a subject, as Lily is in search of her unconscious psyche. All of the characterizations thus far spoken of appear as memory traces; all of these traces eventually emerge into the being that is Lily Briscoe.

In 'The Lighthouse', colours begin to play a more symbolic part of the creative process. The dark browns, violets and purples of the first painting in 'The Window' give way to blues and greens in 'The Lighthouse': blue and green – the imagination and reality, respectively. Lily struggles to recognize these colours as they present themselves, and then begins to utilize them for their symbolic content. This content was prevalent in *The Fisherman's Wife*, where the changing, darkening colours of the sea and sky illustrated the conflict; in Lily's case, the blues and greens assumed predominance as her imagination rises from her unconscious to allow an understanding of the reality in which she has been living for a number of years.

Throughout 'The Lighthouse', Woolf continued to insert herself into the novel, much as Bergman did in *Persona*. Tansley is constantly whispering male chauvinist remarks to Lily[24] early in the novel, a phrase that recurs often enough to become a leitmotif with its constant repetitive insult. In a sense, Woolf is addressing her creative development during the post-Victorian era in Bloomsbury.

Mrs Ramsay, with whom Lily struggled throughout the novel, represented the mother that was never mentioned. At times, Mrs Ramsay fulfils some aspect of a historic absence of feminine energy in Lily's life; I would assume, however, that Mrs Ramsay's animus projections would have led to part of the conflict Lily faced. The need for femininity and animus projection would have, by their nature, created a tension of opposites.

Both Mrs Ramsay and Lily were, at various times, in love with William Bankes. It was Bankes with whom Mrs Ramsay was in love when she accepted Mr Ramsay's proposal. And Lily probably had an affair with Bankes at a later date. Mrs Ramsay was continually stressing that marriage is what every woman needs, particularly to Lily, while simultaneously noting her poor prospects in that area. This formed another obstacle for Lily to overcome, as she finally did by means of recognition of the issue, and which she finalized in her painting.

Lily's struggle to both understand and free herself formed the dramatic, last part of her emergence. At the beginning of 'The Lighthouse', she asked herself the existential question regarding the meaning of life.[25] To answer this, she had to answer her calling – to paint. She performed the ritual of setting up her easel and gathering her supplies. She chose a clean canvas; the old painting of ten years previous was gone. She constantly struggled with the basic parameters of the spatial medium in which she was working: space, mass and perspective. The colours came as a response to the dictates of her unconscious mood. Perspective was also associated with the simultaneous reality of Ramsay's voyage to the lighthouse; his boat diminishes in importance while Lily's painting increases.

The 'ritual' of understanding the process of creativity, which is of primary importance to this discussion of *To the Lighthouse*, can be described by following the thread. At breakfast, at the beginning of 'The Lighthouse', Lily sat alone; St Ives was not what it was ten years previously. Several people had died, primarily

Mrs Ramsay. Gazing at the tablecloth, its pattern reminded her that, at the dinner concluding the day in 'The Window', she had – while looking at that same pattern – thought about her painting, particularly the placement of the tree. This unconscious call from the past was the catalyst for Lily to paint once again. This was Lily's powerful call to action, a life-changing event; Lily was to somehow become an artist. To do so meant to re-prioritize – to follow her own pathway from the consciousness of the technicalities of painting into her inner world: why was the placement of the tree important? And what was the tree?

The morning that 'The Lighthouse' began with the existential question,[26] Lily was immediately catapulted into the past, to the tablecloth revelation, occurring moments later.

Memory had been unleashed. We found Lily burrowing her way over the tablecloth, into her work. At one crucial point, we found colours from the rising sunlight and the sounds of the ocean seemingly uttering other colours.[27] Immediately after, we experience a creative moment that drove her to move the tree to the middle of the painting – in her personal symbolism – to remain unmarried.[28] And then, the meaning of Mrs Ramsay's control over everything, and everyone, sprang into her consciousness, directly from her unconscious.[29] The combining of the colours, and the swirling activity announced that alchemy had led her directly to connection and revelation.[30]

Medieval fires blending many threads – metaphors transitioning into meanings – Lily's grasp of reality opened the pathway to her unconscious by means of her alchemical processes of hollowing and tunnelling through her experiences at St Ives.

> *The alchemists, Jung realized, were, without knowing it, making use of the same mechanism: alchemy was an elaborate discipline based entirely upon the psychological phenomenon of projection.*[31]

As the simultaneous realities of Ramsay's voyage and Lily's painting began to accelerate and finally to coalesce, Ramsay reached his destination, acknowledging the maturity of his son James. And Lily looked at her painting: instinctively, Lily drew a line in the centre of the picture – she had finished – her vision was concluded.

References

1 Lee, H. *Virginia Woolf.* New York: Vintage, 1999, p. 12.
2 Woolf, V. *To the Lighthouse.* New York: Quality Paperback Book Club, 1992, p. 3.
3 'The fisherman and his wife'. In *The Complete Grimm's Fairy Tales.* New York: Random House, 1972, p. 103.
4 Campbell, J. *The Hero with a Thousand Faces.* New York: MFJ Books, 1949, p. 59.
5 Ibid., p. 60.
6 Woolf, p. 119.
7 Ibid., p. 23.
8 Ibid., p. 37.

9 Joyce, J. *Ulysses*. New York: Modern Library, 1942, p. 768.
10 Woolf, p. 165.
11 Ibid., p. 204.
12 Albee, E. *Who's Afraid of Virginia Woolf?* New York: Penguin, 1983.
13 von Franz, M. *Animus and Anima in Fairy Tales*. Toronto: Inner City Books, 2002, p. 17.
14 Sharp, D. *C.G. Jung Lexicon*. Toronto: Inner City Books, p. 23.
15 von Franz, p. 22.
16 Cater. N. *Electra*. New Orleans, LA: Spring, 2003, p. 21.
17 Woolf, p. 198.
18 Joyce, p. 768.
19 Woolf, pp. 198–199.
20 Joyce, p. 768.
21 Britten, B. *Peter Grimes*, Opera 23. London: Boosey & Hawks, 1944.
22 Debussy, C. *Pelléas & Mélisande*. Paris: E. Fromont, 1994.
23 Woolf, p. 80.
24 Ibid., p. 48.
25 Ibid., p. 145.
26 Ibid., p. 146.
27 Ibid., p. 175.
28 Ibid., p. 176.
29 Ibid., p. 175.
30 Ibid.
31 Ibid., p. 209.

9

THE FISHER KING AND THE HANDLESS MAIDEN

Prelude to the *Alexandria Quartet*

Each artistic medium that I have discussed has presented a unique opportunity for the audience to join the creative artist along their pathways; the audience is a critical part of the creative process. I want to now explore the question of origins of the pathways, to see where they are common to all arts, and to all artists.

This study began with the fundamental concept that the creative arts bring the unconscious psyche into consciousness. All of the pathways have that journey in common. This chapter looks at the opportunity presented by the transformation, via art, within both the creator and the artefact; I am speaking, once again, of the concept of X. I repeat: the stirring within the unconscious psyche, for creative artists, is a challenge to explore – to cross a threshold into a new realm; it is this exploration that is the answer to the question of *what* is stirring. This is the catalyst for the work of art. How far can we journey into the unconscious? Is there a fundamental point from which everything grows? Yes – the archetype, and the archetypal images that we have been encountering throughout the previous chapters.

The focus of the next chapter will be Lawrence Durrell's *Alexandria Quartet.*[1,2,3,4] At its conscious foundation, the *Quartet* is complete in four separate but related novels' search for the meaning of love. Complexities that embroider the search with various elaborations and diversions, articulated by a diverse group of characters, manifest themselves throughout the novels. One of the most important threads that weaves throughout is that, in one way or another, they are all wounded. This image has a life of its own.

As prelude to the Durrell novels, I will first follow the thread of being wounded through Robert Johnson's study in *The Fisher King and the Handless Maiden*. He begins with this sentence:

> *This book is about our wounded feeling function, probably the most common and painful wound which occurs in our Western world.*[5]

As he developed his thoughts on the wounded male (the Fisher King) and the wounded female (the Handless Maiden) the previously discussed wounds to both body and psyche began to emerge as a unifying thread among many characters: Nicole Divers in *Tender is the Night*, Alma and Elizabeth in *Persona*, Frida Kahlo, the entire ensemble in *Saraband*, Mr and Mrs Ramsay in *To the Lighthouse*, Munch's melancholia, Beethoven's deafness and Mahler's heart (the ensemble of characters in the *Alexandria Quartet* will be discussed later). In all of these cases, the characters have lost what Johnson terms 'the feeling function', a concept articulated by Jung but used in a slightly different manner by Johnson and others.

In Johnson's book, the unconscious psyche is manifested through the myth of the grail legend and the fairy tale of the handless maiden. (The mythological use of a fairy tale was discussed in Chapter 8.)

> *We may be grateful for the mythology of the twelfth century* [Fisher King/Parsifal], *when so much of our modern world was beginning, for its wounding and final healing.*[6]
>
> *As with all stories and myths, the greatest value* [Handless Maiden] *is in its inner dimensions.*[7]
>
> *Only myth, or art can hold a matter so profound as feeling.*[8]

Because both narratives emerge from the unconscious, I am focusing on that part of Chapter 2 where the process of codifying the X image occurs, before the learned process of the creative medium occurs.

Johnson separates male from female woundings. The Fisher King, the prevailing patriarchal consciousness, is impotent; the Handless Maiden is helpless, unable to do anything for herself or, eventually, her baby. She is a victim of her parents' Faustian bargain, which is ultimately the outcome of industrialization . . . similar to the Fisher King's useless quest for power. Neil Postman presents the history and present dysfunction of the Western world in *Technopoly*.[9] The Faustian bargain of the Handless Maiden's parents is a different quest for power to that of the Fisher King, but they both illustrate how the contemporary Western world's continual pain has morphed from these early manifestations of control, for power, for greed. Thus, we find ourselves in societies without a feeling function; the symptom of these morphed stories that we experience is pain.

> *The meaning of life is not the quest for power or advancement, but lies in the service of that which is greater than one's self.*[10]

The healing of the Fisher King's wound is achieved when Parsifal answers the question: 'Whom does the Grail serve?' This search for the Holy Grail is completed when the Fisher King provides the simple answer: 'It serves the Fisher King' – that is, God.

The innocent fool, Parsifal, has been given two chances to answer the question, thereby releasing the Fisher King from the nearly perpetual pain caused by his wounding. The two meetings between them were separated by many years. At the first meeting, Parsifal does not ask the question; he is undifferentiated, still bound to his mother, unaware of his own psyche.

There are other examples in literature of impotence caused by wounds. From the First World War, Jake Barnes in *The Sun Also Rises* and Clifford (Lord) Chatterley *in Lady Chatterley's Lover*: both are novels that demonstrate the futility of war – the beginnings of industrialized warfare. The D.H. Lawrence novel, in particular, illustrates the clash between nature, the gamekeeper Mellors who lives in the forested park where the sexual, life-affirming events occur, and industrialization, the physically impotent and emotionally sterile owner of the polluting coalmines. These novels are direct illustrations of Johnson's book:

> *Only too often the cultural man (head) kills the natural man (heart) and nature replies by making the cultural man impotent.*[11]

Fishing – inner work – is the only activity that partially relieves the Fisher King's suffering; his healing is the goal of the story. His wounded genital area served the function of the regaining of consciousness; the pain disappeared immediately upon Parsifal's asking the question. The wound itself was a preparation for consciousness.

> *To dethrone anything from consciousness to the unconscious is to diminish it to the status of symptom.*[12]
>
> *. . . consciousness, diminished (sublimated/depressed) into the unconscious . . . morphing into symptom . . . re-emerging as neurosis . . . manifesting as a wound.*
>
> *A true myth always prescribes for the problem that it lays forth. Like any great work of art, it follows the pattern of darkness being redeemed by light.*[13]

'Darkness being redeemed by light' – this is a description of the power of the Romantic impulse, which also encompasses the music of Beethoven and Mahler.

Because of the simplicity of the fairy tale framework, the Handless Maiden appears to be more complex than the myth of the Fisher King. Whereas Parsifal is a product of the medieval chivalric culture where power is the ultimate goal, the maiden in the fairy tale exists in a historical setting that extends further back in time – a product of the collective unconscious – to the spreading of the rhizome from which the archetypal images flourished.

The fairy tale we are discussing illustrates a patriarchal culture with masculinity as villain. Impotence, a male power function, is a wound to the feeling function. The wound to the maiden is different. Although it, too, is the result of a violent action, it is not her generative capacity that is wounded; she is the victim of a far more sinister culture, one that has continued to develop and regenerate for thousands of years, and has become the industrialized world.

Johnson's opening sentence, dealing with 'the most common and painful wound' of our twentieth/twenty-first centuries, requires some interdisciplinary expansion:

> *Industrialization . . . put an end to our medieval manufacture (work by hand) . . . time changed forever . . . transformation from small-scale personalized, skilled labor to large-scale impersonal mechanized production – we had learned how to invent things and the question of why we invent things receded in importance.*[14]

As it progressed, industrialization became the equivalent of dehumanization. This is what happened in the fairy tale discussed. As his fee, the devil took the maiden; her parents consented. The Faustian bargain that followed was a blending of industrialization within the patriarchy from its inception, with mechanization based upon greed, the reward of handlessness, as the price paid. Masculine power triumphs over feminine innocence:

> *To buy material comfort at the cost of feeling values is the devil's bargain.*[15]

The girl's parents are guilty of scapegoating their daughter.[16] Their guilt extends far into the maiden's life. Alice Miller describes the narrative from the point in infancy where the baby is denied love and attention, thereby creating a condition of anxiety and depression that is perpetuated not only throughout the child's life, but also extends into following generations. (Consider the life and turmoil of Virginia Woolf: 'Any person who destroys human life renders himself guilty.'[17])

Writing about her own abuse as a child, Miller adds:

> *At the slightest resistance on my part to my mother's abuse I would have had to fear the direst punishments; and besides having to remain silent, I had to repress my memories and deaden my feelings.*[18]

This, too, is the life the Handless Maiden lived, until her unconscious psyche could burst forth.

The devil's payment for bringing wealth to her parents was the hands of the maiden, which he chopped off and took with him. Masculinity is described as evil;

'a mechanical advance has been won at the expense of the young feminine'.[19] The maiden lived with her now-wealthy parents, and everything was provided for her, with the exception of love, which she had never received as an infant either. She became bored and ultimately depressed. And then came the shift – she ran away, crossing the threshold on her path to individuation.

Like Parsifal, the maiden enters a forest . . . the unconscious psyche. It is here that the maiden will find the solution to her depression, the symptom of the repressed feelings of her early years. Her quest leads her to a lush garden that contains a pear tree; she is back in Eden. (Thus far, the heroic journeys of Parsifal and the maiden are similar.) She is befriended by the garden's owner, with whom she falls in love.

> *He (garden owner/king/husband) unwittingly provided the pears that saved the life of the handless maiden, and now he provided her with silver hands . . . . But note that one gift was natural, the other unnatural . . . it is only an artificial repair, even though it works well for a time.*[20]

She has a baby. The depression returns; she cannot feel the baby with her silver hands. The baby accidentally falls into a stream, and the maiden/now queen, must save her. She weeps, and as she does so, her tears serve a restorative function, turning the mechanical hands once again into flesh and blood. She is able to save her baby. The feeling function, the feminine, returned to her at the most important moment in her life. She had broken, with her tears, the link with her parents', with industrialization's cruelty. Her feeling function was fully restored by the most significant feeling we humans share . . . love.

Interlude: Industrialization as seen by Antonioni and Lawrence

The opening scene of Antonioni's *Red Desert*:[21] Pollution hangs in the air, as if frozen in space; images are black and white, but flames belching from smokestacks are in colour; constant industrial noise, intermingled with electronic music. From a dense cloud of dirty air, colourful Giulliana emerges in a beautiful green coat.

Giulliana reflects the earth's agony as her own . . . an introjection . . . a loss of her feeling function. She suffers from PTSD, has attempted suicide, and is caught between a beautiful world of fantasy and the stark reality of an industrial nightmare. Her alienation is present in a Chirico-like dream, which bears a striking resemblance to two of Professor Borg's dream sequences in Bergman's *Wild Strawberries*. It is as if she cannot distinguish fantasy from reality, but somehow knows she must 'readjust' to reality. And yet, she also feels separated from her own body.

The film is largely without people, only isolated individuals; intimacy and inter–connection do not exist. Feeling is absent. Landscapes are an ecological disaster and human relationships are a cultural disaster. Nature and humanity are enmeshed – the past beauty and fertility of nature has become the shadow of civilization

. . . the industrialized sterility of the present, a time without feeling . . . 'the most common and painful wound which occurs in our Western world'.[22]

The world that Antonioni visualized is similar to the compartmentalized landscape of Lawrence's *Lady Chatterley's Lover*.[23] The dark soot and putrid air of the coalmine community, home of the miners and their families, is in bold contrast to the Chatterley estate. This estate, owned by the industrialist Lord Clifford Chatterley with his wife Connie, includes a wooded area. It is in these woods that Connie meets the gamekeeper, Mellors, with whom she awakens sexually, falls in love and becomes pregnant.

The power of physical love became the power of feeling, for both Connie and Mellors. Connie overcame the entrapment of her mechanized world. Giulliana could not overcome her dissociation. For Connie, she found her reality within her unconscious psyche upon entering the woods.

Like the Fisher King, Clifford was wounded in his genitals, and was impotent; he, too, is unable to walk. The loss of his feeling function permeates the Chatterley estate. Connie is eventually overcome with the pollution emanating from Clifford, and also loses feeling. The world of the industrialist is sterile, while that of the woods, of Mellors, is verdant and fertile. Connie eventually rejects sterility in crossing the threshold of the woods; through her sexual awakening, she regains her feeling function – beginning life anew.

A feeling is as indisputable a reality as the existence of an idea.[24]

I have presented various parts of a framework for the reality that is the loss of the feeling function – the ability to feel. Whatever the mixture of physical and emotional woundings, the wound itself serves as a catalyst for action. Typically, such a catalyst acts as a calling that precedes the beginning of the hero's journey, as clearly described in Campbell's *Hero with a Thousand Faces*.[25]

To proceed on the journey is to answer the call: Connie Chatterley did, and continued her journey to individuation. Giulliana did not, and continued on her path of neurosis. She sought a rebirth of her feeling function from a sexual encounter with a man to whom she attempted to be attracted.

Connie succeeded where Giulliana did not. Her reality with Mellors, their emotional bonding, was their mutual sexual attraction. This bonding . . . this feeling . . . preceded their words. Connie was the one who entered the woods.

Giulliana did not succeed. She did not take action on her own, could not cross a threshold. Her lover could not fulfil the catalytic function of bringing her to take action and live with him . . . which was, in itself, an action. She could not choose between the colourful world that was her unconscious psyche and the outer, despoiled world. She remained in place, while Connie began her journey.

Some wounds can be healed; others cannot. What determines the result is the process upon which various persons journey. There are many helpers along the way. As I hope I have suggested, many present a threshold through the creative arts.

References

1 Durrell, L. *Justine*. New York: Dutton, 1958.
2 Durrell, L. *Balthazar*. New York: Dutton, 1958.
3 Durrell, L. *Mountolive*. New York: Dutton, 1959.
4 Durrell, *Clea*. New York: Dutton. 1960.
5 Johnson, R. *The Fisher King and the Handless Maiden*. San Francisco, CA: HarperCollins, 1995, p. 3.
6 Ibid., p. 48.
7 Ibid., p. 95.
8 Ibid., p. 10.
9 Postman, N. *Technopoly*. New York: Vintage Books, 1993.
10 Johnson, p. 46.
11 Ibid., p. 21.
12 Ibid., p. 32.
13 Ibid., p. 36.
14 Postman, pp. 40–43.
15 Johnson, p. 62.
16 Ibid., p. 64.
17 Miller, A. *Banished Knowledge: Facing Childhood Injuries*. New York: Anchor Books, 1990, p. 20.
18 Ibid., p. 15.
19 Johnson, p.59.
20 Ibid., p. 85.
21 Antonioni, M. (Dir.). *Red Desert*. Film Duemila, 1964.
22 Johnson, p. 3.
23 Lawrence, D.H. *Lady Chatterley's Lover*. New York: Signet Classics, 2003.
24 Jung, C. *The Practice of Psychotherapy, Collected Works 16*, Para. 53.
25 Campbell, J. *The Hero with a Thousand Faces*. New York: MFJ Books, 1949.

10

THE *ALEXANDRIA QUARTET*

Lawrence Durrell describes his novel in four parts, the *Alexandria Quartet*, as a study in love, in its modern sense.[1] There are two forerunners to the *Quartet*: Plato's *Symposium*, because it discusses the same subject – the meaning of love[2] and de Sade's *Justine*, because it shares the same title, and is often quoted by Durrell.[3] Plato investigates the meaning of love in a manner consistent with thought in fourth-century BCE Greece. De Sade's novel (1798) is more useful for this chapter, even though its subject is an ongoing definition of evil. However, it is the construction of this novel that is relevant to our discussion.

The reality of de Sade's addiction to the subject of evil leads to an interesting deepening of the subject of love. Lyn Cowan writes:

> *The authentic Eros is truly a god, a divinity of power, passion, and range. As one of the soul's prime movers, he is capable of cruel as well as compassionate love . . . Sometimes in our relatedness we suffer a wounding and a tearing apart. This is Eros, too, perhaps what we may call a sadistic Eros.*[4]

She broadens the issue:

> *In this mythic story, it is the return of desire (Eros) that rescues the soul (Psyche) from its suicidal despair.*[5]

Eros, the Greek personification of love, is not a singular, unidirectional god-figure. He is far more complex; love itself is far more complex. As we shall see in the *Quartet*, it is so richly nuanced as to often reach a point vastly different from its origin. In searching for a definition of love, there is a question of whether these conclusions we reach, the characters that live, are points of opposition to or an extension of our initial encounters with them: their points of origin in the narratives.

This is not an academic question, for these two terms – opposition versus extension – pose an issue that occupies Durrell throughout the novels. The term 'opposite' presumes polarity, an identity far removed from the initial point of origin – our first encounter with each character, with nothing shared between this and the encounters that unfold in the narrative; it is, in a sense, the depth psychological concept 'shadow'. The term 'extension' implies an unfolding from a point of origin while retaining that point; it is shared with its origin, not requiring oppositional positioning, but is only a nuance, and variation or elaboration of the original: a non-psychological concept.

Cowan presents the issue of the meaning of Eros that is a refinement of the myth that we tend to accept, based upon a highly popular, even commercial, version. We are provided with a key to understanding one of the complex threads of the structure and content of Durrell's brilliant and poetic *Alexandria Quartet*: the dissociative element in love as seen by some of the characters.

Durrell quotes de Sade at the beginning of each of the four novels. He shares more than the title with de Sade. It is the wounding and tearing apart that is a common theme to both authors. Durrell is far more sophisticated on the theme of love than is de Sade on the theme of evil. De Sade's novel simply alternates between late eighteenth-century philosophical discourse and brutal sexual violence against Justine. Even with these alternating sections, it is a unidirectional study ... that ultimately comes full circle without being on a journey. The clever banalities of the philosophical arguments, which always coalesce into justifications for sexual sadism, lead me to question the non-cumulative goal of this type of structure; it has no progress, and time is measured by points on a clock rather than accomplishment of an artistic goal. We eventually know more about sadism than we do about evil.

Initially, it is difficult to understand Durrell's use of de Sade. However, there is a de Sade quote at the beginning of *Balthazar* that provides some meaningful insight. It articulates differences among mirrors and what they may affect.[6] Mirrors are frequently used in the *Alexandria Quartet* as commentaries or points of view. (I will discuss this soon.) But it is the nature of opposites of the vision itself – beautiful versus frightful – that provides the insight into Durrell.

The ever-present naiveté of de Sade's Justine bears a peculiar relationship to the continual uncertainties of Durrell's Justine. The former is repeatedly sexually abused by the men with whom she comes in contact; the latter continually wounds those with whom she is having affairs. De Sade's character is the product of simple religious beliefs; Durrell's character, the victim of a traumatic series of events and an existentially hostile environment, cannot combine intimacy with sex. Both characters show an inability to discern what is meaningful to their respective psyches: differentiation. Differentiation is the separation of parts from the whole.

> *Undifferentiated thinking is incapable of thinking apart from other functions . . . Without differentiation direction is impossible, since the direction of a function towards a goal depends on the elimination of anything irrelevant. Fusion with the irrelevant precludes direction; only a differentiated function is capable of being directed.*[7]

Both Justines exhibit self-destructive, undifferentiated behaviours. While the patterns of behaviour are different – one passive, the other passive-aggressive – the detachment from love and intimacy is similar. De Sade's Justine is constantly being physically assaulted, while Durrell's Justine has a propensity for emotionally assaulting. Regardless of the type of assault and its direction (male to female or vice versa), damage is pervasive.

Both Clea and Darley are participants in Durrell's version of the Justine characters' confused and confusing lives, lives without differentiation, which is impossible for them. De Sade's character is without nuance or dimension. But in Durrell's, we find an examination of the nuanced complexities of modern (twentieth-century) love, together with an anticipation of a resolution – a differentiation – of these complexities, as the writer subtly constructs his narrative.

At one time or another, all of Durrell's characters reflect upon love. In *Justine*, the paradox of that which unites is also described as that which may divide, with equal power in both directions.[8]

Darley, one of the main characters – the voice of Durrell – labels this paradox a *boustrophedon*: an ancient method of writing where the lines alternated right to left, then left to right. This is a linkage between cyclic structure in writing and the musical structure that uses leitmotifs . . . and the subject of love. Another paradox appears – strength as an individual's power, which can equally serve to deter.[9]

Durrell presents the notion that Justine's powerful animus interferes with Eros: non-differentiation . . . or the Shadow? Perhaps this is a reference to one of the structural features of moving partitions, and the paradox of love's potential for loneliness.[10]

Pursewarden is the *Quartet*'s archetypal image of the philosopher/artist. Here is one of his views on love – the cynical side. This blends with Nessim's question regarding his marriage to Justine, where love is a Faustian bargain. It suggests a contractual element in love relationships for those not yet truly committed to one another.[11]

Pursewarden had a lengthy affair with his blind sister, Lisa, introducing incest as a complexity of love; such complexities will ultimately evolve into musical structure. Eventually, Pursewarden could no longer live with his guilt; to free Lisa, he committed suicide, realizing that neither would be able to have a meaningful love life with a different person.[12]

Darley and Clea are bonding throughout the first three novels, their love for each other emerging in the fourth, but not fully realized until their final exchange of letters at the conclusion of *Clea*. In *Balthazar*, Clea inquires of Darley as to whether the bond of love is one that causes a wounding.[13]

Assertion as question: vulnerability is not often expressed in the *Quartet*. It is one of the powerful influences that eventually lead the two to each other. In this particular passage, we experience honesty in the form of vulnerability, as if Clea is seeking her feeling function. But, the presence of Clea and Darley in this narrative is, in the end, the opposite of the modern love that Durrell is attempting to understand. The focus of Durrell's quest is, allusively, Justine, for she is the central figure around whom all the characters orbit; only Darley and Clea can eventually break away from her. This is not to say that Justine is without attraction, or without the capacity to attract men who would be healers. This need for a healer is based upon her history of being raped as a teenager, which had lasting consequences for many years.[14]

In addition, her child (not from the rape) was stolen from her many years ago. Nessim, her unloved husband through most of the *Quartet*, devoted a great deal of time and money unsuccessfully trying to find the child. The ongoing tension of Justine's not knowing her child's fate, and the projection of her anxieties upon all who knew her, created a sympathetic character. She was a Jew, married to a Copt – both of whom were involved in the creation of the State of Israel in 1948. This marriage, a Faustian bargain, is one of the complex of threads running throughout the novels. Just before their marriage, Nessim reflects upon Justine's need for power.[15]

The characters represent, symbolically, the plethora of concepts of love that Durrell found in Alexandria: straight, gay, prostitutes, gigolo, young man/older woman, lovers in need of healing and healing lovers. They are all 'modern'; only Clea and Darley fail to represent that designation, in their romantic love.

In Johnson's book on the feeling function (see Chapter 9), the wounds of which he spoke were physical metaphors for powerful disturbances of the psyche. In the beginning of *Justine*, psychic wounds were not as immediately obvious as they are in the myth or fairy tale. But the physical wounds were present almost from the introduction of each character: Justine (PTS, victim of rape), Melissa (TB), Lisa (blind), Leila (smallpox), Semira (no nose), Nessim (war wounds), Mountolive (epilepsy), Narouz (hare lip), Balthazar (illness unspecified), Pursewarden (eventual suicide) – and, of course, Darley, whose creative block/loss of feeling, is one of the central threads of the *Quartet*, eventually intertwining with Clea (who has lost a hand in an accident) to narrow to the central thread of the quartet.

Darley's loss profoundly affects his generative function, which is symbolized by his creative block. In Clea's case, similar to that of Lily Briscoe, the acquisition of the creativity within her unconscious psyche resulted from an acceptance of X. Each experienced a moment of confrontation with a deep-seated calling from her unconscious – each answered the call. Being wounded allows the unconscious psyche to break into consciousness, in these cases (Darley, Clea, Lily Briscoe) manifested through the creative arts.

Darley has wrapped his narrative of the wounds of modern love in the context of Alexandria and environs. At the beginning of *Justine*, he describes Alexandria as the generative force, as the foundation of wounded love, a place where the sexual wounding of men occurred.[16]

The sick men who have been deeply wounded in their sex are similar to the Fisher King. Although the quote is confined to men, there is much intense suffering by many of the *Quartet*'s female characters. However, the feminine wounds are not in their genitals. It is interesting to speculate if Durrell was attempting to propose a difference between female suffering, in their psyche, as opposed to male suffering, in their genitals. I do not think this is necessarily the case: first, the character of Justine is a character with a powerful animus and, second, because both Darley and Clea were able to integrate the other's anima. They were the only characters able to do so . . . but then again, they were the only characters able to break the boundaries of modern love, as Durrell defined it.

★

At the beginning of this chapter, I mentioned Plato's *Symposium* as one of the forerunners of Durrell's *Quartet*. The dialogue is an interesting exploration of the meaning of love, seen from a lengthy historical/cultural distance. The contribution of Aristophanes is particularly germane. Campbell provides some interesting insight into this work.[17]

★

Johnson led me into the fabric and inner chambers of the *Alexandria Quartet*. Durrell extends the Jungian concepts of myth and fairy tale, upon which Johnson concentrated, onto a broader landscape – almost a novel of ideas, but certainly an inductive dialogue with the author. The prevailing consciousness of the archetypes are filtered through the lens of Alexandria. They are, naturally, more complex as they grow into a tapestry of narratives . . . but that is their nature, as seen in the reference to organic structure in Beethoven. Ultimately, the archetypes return in their original format, at the end of *Clea*. The principle of return, a cornerstone of Romanticism, is articulated with immensely powerful and emotional honesty by Gustav Mahler. The final step to Mahler is to achieve an understanding of the structure of the *Alexandria Quartet*.

The structure of the *Alexandria Quartet*

Two threads, which have recurred throughout these chapters in one form or another, will be followed in order to reach an understanding of the structure of these novels. They are: first, how a structure is created to integrate the various thematic elements and, second, how does this structure aspire to Pater's premise about music. We shall see that the two threads are woven together, for they lead back to, and are therefore derived from, the same point of origin: the leitmotif, derived from music, leads to music.

The structure of the *Alexandria Quartet*, a novel in four parts, is similar to the symphonies of Mahler, a symphony in 10 parts; they both rely upon memory, either in words or notes, to create structure. Constant recurrences, unannounced but remembered, bind these works of art into continuous if segmented wholes. At every motivic recurrence, memory is activated. These memories broaden and deepen the motif until it begins to transcend consciousness, penetrating the unconscious. It becomes a structure by accretion, a point where the threads we have been pursuing reach their point of origin. Since the motivic repetitions are both irregular and unpredictable, how do we find meaning?

In his introduction to Freud's *Dora: Analysis of a Case of Hysteria*, Rieff refers to Freud as a 'spiritual detective'.[18] Freud himself describes his deductive process with Dora, making the point:

> *consecutive presentation is not a very adequate means of describing mental processes going on in different layers of the mind.*[19]
>
> *the juxtaposition of the most dissimilar tendencies, the mutual dependence of contrary ideas, the placements and displacements . . . the idee fixe . . .*[20]

Hillman refers to Dora in a similar way:

> *these detective-story-style appeals to reason, reminding him (the reader) of what was said some pages back, or cautioning him that Dora was a case study of the symptom of hysteria, a different sort of message from her unconscious than those, in the creative arts, with which we have been involved. The recurrences, or memories solicited by the detective-story technique, lead us back to the archetypes.*[21]

In *Re-visioning Psychology*, Hillman quotes Plotinus:

> *all knowing comes by likeness and describes this phenomenon . . . the idea that all things desire to return to the archetypal originals of which they are copies and from which they proceed.*[22]

Repeating an earlier thought: in this context, Durrell is referring to one of the complexities of Darley's relationship, the *boustrophedon*, in a more sophisticated manner; the paradox of love as both a binding and breaking element, mentioned here, again.[23]

The paradox is drawn from the image. It is a form of mirror, one that obliterates space and time, for neither is meaningful when viewed from the interior of the design.

Throughout the *Alexandria Quartet*, mirrors are used to decipher impressions that move between appearance and reality, conscious images and unconscious psyche. It is in this uncertainty, this tension between what is perceived and what is felt, that the depth of the characters unfolds. This unfolding is the journey itself.

To extend this idea: perhaps, in the midst of the journey, we cannot locate ourselves – our present. We know the past, and fantasize the future. But from within a work of art, we need the guidance of the creator of that work in our process of de-coding what has been placed before us.

Another way of describing this phenomenon, particularly of the elasticity of the spatial and temporal dimensions as seen through the mirror, occurs early in the first novel; Justine, gazing through a set of mirrors, can envision multiple parts of her being simultaneously: her psyche.[24]

This is both a perfect description of Justine and of the general structure of the *Quartet*. Characters are continually looking at themselves and/or are seen in mirrors. Impressions and interpretations of life, both lived and imagined, are censored by projected images. Justine's quotation reflects how the mosaic that is the *Alexandria Quartet* is constructed . . . simultaneous imagery.

In returning to Pater's thesis, an old question suggests a new frame. 'What does art itself create?'[25] Langer's question applies to all arts, proposing and simultaneously deepening the assumption that it is the artist alone who creates the artefact. While the assumption is literally true, there is a dynamic, discussed in Chapter 1, which places an additional focus on the assumption. Langer's point is that art creates feelings – emotions based upon responses. Feeling, in this context and as I have been using it, is an emotional response derived from contact with the unconscious. In Langer's many books, we systematically study precisely how this process comes about, from symbolization through to its ultimate conclusion in our feeling response.

> *Music is the tonal analogue of our emotional life.*[26]

This is a refinement from an earlier quote, substituting 'tonal' for 'symbolic'.[27] But the use of the musical term inserts her formulation directly into Pater's concept.

It is not only Durrell who is placing the motifs sporadically throughout the *Alexandria Quartet*, it is mainly the reader who is placing them into a coherent/memory-based structure. This is exactly what occurs in music, and is Pater's idea brought to life. Amidst the *idée fixe* of Berlioz and the leitmotif of Wagner, it is the 'condition of music'.

*

At one point in their relationship, Clea says to Darley that she wanted to reconstruct the city for him.[28] The city of Alexandria had undergone an evolution similar to many of the characters – disintegration and death. It was a powerful part of the action of the *Quartet*. It was lush and vibrant – decaying – decadent. Like the characters in the novels, the city never reconciled its opposites. As a city, as a population, it had lost its feeling function. The conflicts there had morphed into someplace else; the city of love[29] had become a whore.[30]

Towards the end of *Clea*, Darley writes to Clea that, were it not for her, he would not return to Alexandria, so much had it changed.[31] And then, Darley pivots, crossing the threshold to his journey. The Romanticism towards which Durrell had been moving throughout the *Alexandria Quartet* emerges; he has decided to turn westward towards old Europe, something that, we will finally surmise with the entire set of novels before us, is Romanticism – which includes a life with Clea.[32]

Darley/Durrell is recapturing the function of his feeling, healing his wound, rejecting a painful part of his past by integrating it into his present, as a catalyst for his future, as did Dick Divers. And Clea, like Lily Briscoe, paints, the new-found feeling pulsing through her prosthetic hand, unconscious psyche finally born to art. While the other central characters remained in Alexandria, Clea and Darley had finally found each other; they were now able to begin their journey together.

Clea finally emerges as the painter she had wished to become. And Darley begins his novel with the words drawn from the unconsciousness of the universal fairy tale – Once upon a time . . . .[33]

References

1 Durrell, L. *Balthazar*. New York: Dutton, 1958, p. 2.
2 Plato. *The Dialogues of Plato*, Vol. I. M. Jowett (trans). New York: Random House, 1937, pp. 318–319.
3 Sade, M. de. *Justine; or Good Conduct Well-Chastised*. P. Casavini (trans). Paris: Olympia Press, 1963.
4 Cowan, L. *Masochism: A Jungian View*. Woodstock, NY: Spring, 1997, p. 59.
5 Cowan, L. *Portrait of the Blue Lady*. New Orleans, LA: Spring, 2004, p. 150.
6 Durrell, *Balthazar*, p. 3.
7 Jung, C. *Psychological Types, Collected Works 6*, Para. 705.
8 Durrell, L. *Justine*. New York: Dutton, 1958, p. 158.
9 Ibid., p. 50.
10 Durrell, L. *Clea*. New York: Dutton, 1960, p. 64.
11 Durrell, L. *Mountolive*. New York: Dutton, 1959, p. 195.
12 Ibid., p. 173.
13 Durrell, *Balthazar*, p. 236.
14 Ibid., p. 146.
15 Durrell, *Mountolive*, p. 201.
16 Durrell, *Justine*, p. 14.
17 Campbell, J. *The Masks of God: Occidental Mythology*. New York: Penguin, 1976, pp. 226–232.
18 Freud, S. *Dora: An Analysis of a Case of Hysteria*. P. Rieff (ed.). New York: Collier Books, 1979, p. 10.
19 Ibid., p. 9.
20 Ibid., p. 136.
21 Hillman, J. *Healing Fiction*. Woodstock: Spring, 1983, p. 4.
22 Hillman, J. *Re-visioning Psychology*. New York: Harper & Row, 1976, p. 99.
23 Durrell, *Justine*, p. 157.
24 Ibid., p. 27.

25 Langer, S. *Feeling and Form: A Theory of Art*. New York: Scribner, 1953, p. 10.
26 Ibid., p. 27
27 Ibid., p. 40.
28 Durrell, *Clea*, p. 89.
29 Durrell, *Justine*, p. 13.
30 Ibid., p. 14.
31 Durrell, *Clea*, p. 276.
32 Ibid.
33 Ibid., p. 282.

11

GUSTAV MAHLER

The threads that I have pursued throughout this book, as if on a quest, have inexorably led to Romanticism. The great tradition of the creative Romantics held that one's life should be changed by experiencing their art. Theirs was the era in which a new consciousness was emerging – that of exploring the unconscious psyche. Of course, the unconscious psyche, via a plethora of symbolic artefacts, had been in existence for centuries. Durrell's conclusion of his exploration of love ends with the sentence, 'once upon a time', as if it were a fairy tale.

But in the nineteenth century, both in the beginnings of the study of psychology and in the flowering – indeed, the passionate overabundance – of the creative arts, the Romantic epoch began. In music, it began with Beethoven and reached its apex in Mahler.

*

Gustav Mahler represents a unique challenge to those who are intimately involved in the arts, music in particular, and in psychology. To some, he is historically the conclusion of the Romantic era, while to others he is the beginning of the modern era. What is fascinating is that holders of both views generally cite the same works to support their beliefs. Unlike Beethoven, whose work can be conveniently divided into three periods, Mahler's symphonies represent one continuous journey; or, from a more focused position, they represent a continuous attempt to deal with the same material, the same issues perceived from varying points along his journey.

In Mahler, biography is transformed into music, while music is translated into biography; it is from his music that we know his life. His historical position is not ambivalent – he is both the end of Romanticism and the birth of Modernism. He is the epic transitional figure and with the distance of time we may now be in a position to understand him. Freud had put us on the wrong track in terms of psychobiography. What is most difficult to determine in music is a technique for understanding his musical process *per se*, without using theoretical jargon and/or the illusion that analysed numbers yield worthwhile information. As I have tried to show throughout this book, asking questions is choosing which threads to follow.

From the Renaissance until the early twentieth century, point of view in painting referred to perspective. The musical equivalent of perspective arrived in the early Baroque with tonality, assuring music's evolution from a basically horizontal-contrapuntal art to a vertical-harmonic art. Prior to the Renaissance and, in some cases, beginning early in the twentieth century, ordering was the task of the listener. The audience was firmly guided through harmony-derived structures . . . until the time of Wagner. *Tristan and Isolde* changed everything. The opening dissonance went unresolved until the last notes of the opera; time was expanded to a point where the audience had to engage with the music and actively formulate structure. The relationships between dissonance and consonance were reversed, and the *leitmotif*, particularly from his *Ring Cycle*, embellished previous structures. The common syntax of the past 250 years had been reconstructed from its predictable periodicity to a situation in which the audience had to actively participate in structural creation. The composer aided this through motivic repetitions. It worked.

Mahler (1860–1911) had a particular point of view about his music, which transcends the technical. Quite simply, within his symphonies he wanted to create a universe. Most would view this as a grandiose delusion. However, Mahler was not thinking astronomically. His 'universe' was a journey to the far reaches of the self; the unexplored territory was the psyche. The archetypal themes that he explored – life, love, death, resurrection – are all manifestations not of the ego, but of the substance beneath. They are also musically archetypal; most of his thematic content is based on similar pitch choices, and his uses of orchestration and pedal-tone harmonies permeate all of the symphonies.

The Mahler point of view, his soulful perspective, emanates directly from the music itself; it is the documentation we have. For example, the adagietto of his *Symphony No. 5* is a long, continuous gesture, kept alive by the use of pitches that are not part of the harmony occupying predominant rhythmic positions, strongly accented, where previous eras in music used pitches that were part of the harmony. Thus, that which is 'out of place' occupies the most prominent position. This creates a continual source of expectation – that certain pitches will ultimately appear. This expectation is what causes emotional response. It simultaneously retains and subverts rootedness. This is how he creates, technically . . . beyond the censor line in X's upward trajectory. But the point of view from which he creates is something different. In exceeding the limitations of phrasing and roundedness that are synonymous with music of earlier epochs, Mahler is felt to somehow be extending . . . something . . . somewhere. Thus did the twentieth century begin with a new search for beauty, deriving from nineteenth-century harmonic concepts that were recast from a personal point of view.

We search for existential meaning in Mahler's *Symphony No. 2*, which presents us with the duality of life and death, followed by resurrection of the hero who was created in *Symphony No. 1*. This life/death duality is one with which Mahler struggled throughout his entire life. Jung describes this change thus:

> *Out of* [the] *collision of opposites the unconscious psyche always creates a third thing of an irrational nature, which the conscious mind neither expects nor understands. It presents itself in a form that is neither a straight 'yes' nor a straight 'no'.*[1]

This refers to the transcendent function. I suggest that the product, this 'third thing of an irrational nature', is the work of art. This transcendent function must serve as part of the initial process through which X is making symbols.

One of the best examples of Mahler's musical point of view is to be found in the first movement of his *Symphony No. 6*. First, we find a recurring motif, a transition from major to minor triads, reversing the Romantic vision of darkness into light. In this reversal we find a symbolic memory-twist, and something is uttered without preparation. A symbolic process that breaks its direction signals that something is wrong; the disturbance elicits an emotional response.

More important is the thematic blending in the first movement. Mahler has described the first movement's second theme as his 'Alma theme', attempting to musically demonstrate his love for his wife. But consider: the movement begins with a decidedly militaristic, march-like theme. This mood transitions to the lovely, haunting melody of the Alma theme. But, as the Alma theme approaches its last few measures, the militaristic theme returns, as an intrusive counterpoint. While the first theme was allowed to play in its entirety, the second theme is not. Clearly, not all was well in the Mahler household. Mahler was in the midst of a period during which he was composing *Kindertotenlieder* (songs on the death of a child), the actual death of one of his children, his continuing problems with the Viennese opera and the anti-Semitic milieu of the city and, later, his awareness of Alma's infidelity. This general unhappiness found its way into musical expression, perhaps without Mahler consciously realizing it.

Mahler stretched the vision of syntactical rootedness (tonality) as far as it could go. The artistic perspective, in the painter's sense, translated into tonality in the musical sense, was at hand. Debussy took flight from tonality, creating music that is semantically tonal yet without the teleology of harmonic syntax. One need only compare the opening phrases of the Ravel and Debussy string quartets to see this process. While they both use the same tonal structures on the language, Ravel remains rooted in the past in his syntactical use, while Debussy moves his forward into the future. By means of a new syntax, Debussy created a different sense of time, the time of Proust, Joyce . . . and the transduced image into a temporal, frozen setting by Picasso. All this, in turn, created a need for different structures. Mahler's genius felt the need, created a new language out of his found objects, and filled the need by using what he found to explore the vast unknown world . . . within himself.

Mahler's vision left the rootedness of the past while on a journey towards inner space. The dualities of his symphonies, the opposites and the empowering of lyrical symmetry – the subversion of the past was a vision in progress. His quest for the universality of music began with the hero's birth and lasted throughout his *Symphony No. 9*. With his recurring motifs, it is sometimes difficult to determine when a previous symphony ends and the next one begins. It is not that he fails to convincingly conclude each one; rather, it is that the energy which flows throughout never subsides. Each symphony appears as an old friend, a reconnection with the past – Mahler's past, the listener's past. And when the final notes of *Symphony No. 9* have faded – as Leonard Bernstein wrote on the title page of his score of this symphony:

> *The refined beauties of ambiguity . . . The obsessiveness of artistic creation . . . Obsessiveness caused by the urge to produce the perfect form of his 'vision.' If he had lived he might have tried 9 more times.*[2]

Except for the fact that his incomplete *Symphony No. 10* set forth into a new world; perhaps he was already in the stars.

Epilogue

It is not important to know if Pater was correct in his assertion that all arts aspire to the condition of music. What is important is to understand what he was attempting to say. Perhaps some thoughts from an obituary on Claude Lévi-Strauss put Pater's thought into a numinous perspective:

> *With the fading of myth's power in the modern West, he* [Lévi-Strauss] *also suggested that music had taken on myth's function. Music, he argued, had the ability to suggest, with primal narrative power, the conflicting forces and ideas that lie at the foundations of society.*[3]

Lévi-Strauss defines the condition of music as myth-making. Yes! It is the power of the completed cycle of X that reaches into, and beyond, consciousness, into the unconscious psyche, to the very essence of humanity. One needs only to listen to the symphonies of Gustav Mahler to understand what Darley meant in writing 'once upon a time'.

References

1 Jung, C. *The Archetype and the Collective Unconscious*, *Collected Works 9, I*, Para. 285.
2 Wakin, D. 'Mahler said what to whom?' *New York Times*, 14 February 2011, Arts, p. 1.
3 Rothstein, E. 'Claude Levi-Strauss, 100, dies; altered western views of the "primitive"'. *New York Times*, 4 November 2009, p. B16.

PART TWO

The end of boundaries

12

GEORGIA O'KEEFFE

The touch of desire

. . . something remains unexamined . . .

I return to that point in Chapter 7 where I entered the large room in the Gallery of the Soul, a room which symbolizes the depth of the unconscious. Surrounding me are the paintings of Georgia O'Keeffe: landscapes, flowers, bones, abstractions. There are no people in the paintings. Colours and disguised structural forms are vehicles for images that powerfully engage my eyes. I am challenged. The setting feels like some sort of protest.

In the beginning of my O'Keeffe study, I was primarily attracted to the landscapes. It was during this initial acquaintance that I first noticed the lack of human beings or even animals, and found myself asking 'Why nothing alive?' Next, that part of me which asks questions inquired as to why I was asking this particular question. I was searching for a thread.

Experience teaches that imagination is a way in which feelings and emotions are directly communicated. Throughout these discussions, complex offerings have arrived from somewhere within X, causing me to find a way in which to understand what is being 'said'. With O'Keeffe's potent colours swirling around me, with background murmurings – some verbal, most musical – filled the aural and physical space; I felt the colours most forcefully, and realized that this was a thread for which I'd been searching.

Several O'Keeffe landscapes offer the clarity of her vision: *Black Mesa Landscape, New Mexico* (1930), *Charna River, Ghost Ranch* (1937), *Lavender Ghost Ranch* (1935), *Near Abiquiú, New Mexico* (1930), *Road Past the View 1* (1964) and *Gray Hills* (1962) – all are excellent examples of scenes transformed from natural settings to visionary commentaries. What she sees in the landscapes is what exists in her imagination: a vision of a vision.

It is clear that these O'Keeffe landscapes are very different from those of earlier times, such as *Eagle Cliff Franconia Notch* (1864) by David Johnson. Painting from within the historical culture of the day, Johnson represented as precisely as possible the scene he was viewing directly from his vision onto the canvas without mediation from some aspect of his unconscious. This was without that part of X, from Chapter 2, which precedes crossing the boundary between the unconscious and consciousness. This is the part of the journey where technique to articulate is of primary importance. Photography was on the near horizon, but painters were still in the art-as-information period of landscapes and portraits.

O'Keeffe's landscapes do not draw upon the techniques of those mid-nineteenth-century painters. The vision that O'Keeffe presents to us is of a world seemingly never seen. Her New Mexico mountains contain no people, no animals, unlike the earlier landscapists who frequently included some token living being, animal and/or human. There are also no boundaries to either the foreground or background. We 'enter' an O'Keeffe landscape seemingly arriving from a background of forever, and proceed through and out of the setting into infinity:

> *The landscapes of Georgia O'Keeffe present a virgin state of nature, untouched by man.*

In O'Keeffe's United States, virgin landscapes were a reality.

> *Georgia O'Keeffe's connection with the world of romanticism and her pleasure in working with trees and nature . . . born in a country where there were still places untouched by human hand.*[1]

The shapes of O'Keeffe's mountains are easily identifiable as such. But they differ from the particular mountains the paintings are depicting as well as the craggy dramatic shapes of the prototypical with which we are familiar. (We shall address this issue in the writings of Lawrence and Cather.)

The O'Keeffe mountains are usually rounded, as if she were viewing mountains that existed tens of millions of years ago, the water which covered these areas only recently departed. Shapes are identifiable – almost as if they were underwater:

> *Time Present and Time Past.*[2]

Colours present a different, more puzzling problem than the various shapes. Two examples comparing colour photographs with the painting of the same landscape, side by side, illustrate O'Keeffe's subtle blending of pastels and earth tones. These colours are her vision of what she sees; it is important to repeat this idea, because all great works of art, no matter what the medium, are important keys for unlocking the complete psyche of the creative person. The shapes of these visions can be seen in *Black Mesa Landscape, New Mexico*[3] and *The Cliff Chimneys.*[4]

The landscapes are clearly articulated in the paintings, but particularly in the former. It is more difficult to match photos with artwork, because the artistic vision allows for what the painter wants you to see – and the assumption is that there exists a bond of trust between artist and viewer that the latter's expectation of truth has been honoured. So, the colour exchanges that we view are from the natural environment to a very sophisticated palate of colours. Perhaps the smoothing out of the mountains aids O'Keeffe, in part, as a way in which to make the colour differentiation more dramatic: take away the rugged terrain in service to the drama of the colour. The energy created by the painting is thus a projection of colour subdued in service to the shapes.

The colours of O'Keeffe's flowers demonstrate a different mood – perhaps, a different persona from that of the landscapes. In the flowers we experience a dynamic intensity; the landscapes invite us in, while the flowers engulf us, surrounding us, saturating us to the point that we metaphorically become part of the flower. Her fascination with flowers began before her work on landscapes:

> *This was the 1920's, and everything was going so fast. Nobody had time to reflect . . . It was exquisite, but it was so small you really could not appreciate it for itself . . . If I could paint that flower in a huge scale, then you could not ignore its beauty.*[5]

Temporally locating her statement – and, actually her work – in the 1920s places it in the midst of the beginnings of America's entrance into the arts. It is the world we experienced in *Tender is the Night.* In the world of painting, the major figures who were to dominate early twentieth-century art (Picasso, Matisse, Cezanne, etc.) were gaining recognition.

> *Georgia O'Keeffe flirted with abstract art throughout various periods of her artistic life, but never abandoned the representational world.*[6]

But O'Keeffe stood apart from the various schools of thought and movements of painting. She was an avid follower of Kandinski, particularly of his philosophical treatise *Concerning the Spiritual in Art.* The main thrust of Kandinski's discussion is as follows:

> *The artist must have something to say, for mastery over form is not his goal, but rather the adapting of form to its inner meaning.*[7]

In another section:

> *We are seeking today for the road which is to lead us away from the outer to the inner basis.*[8]

Separating the external (reality) from the internal (spiritual), Kandinski is focusing on feeling over form. This is exactly what O'Keeffe meant when she repeated her mantra of wanting to make known the unknown. This was her way of saying that she wanted to bring the unconscious into consciousness. It is for the artist to process their spiritual content into a work of art. This becomes, in itself, a reality –but a reality of the feeling function.

For O'Keeffe, feeling/emotion is represented by her paintings – similar to the other creators I have been discussing. It is important to keep in mind that all artists reach inside, but not all successfully grasp what is there.

It is, however, somewhat difficult to actually experience the emotion in O'Keeffe's work. Emotional expression was something about which she felt deeply. But without social or human content in her works, it is difficult to find a context for emotion. Something in her art must stir something in the viewer.

To begin tracing a new thread of enquiry, we will next explore these same mountains that drew O'Keeffe's attention and functioned similarly, to a degree, in works by D.H. Lawrence and Willa Cather.

The reason for choosing Lawrence and Cather is that most of the books discussed were set in the same terrain that O'Keeffe painted; and many of the paintings were created in close temporal proximity to each other. Thinking about the words and the paintings, simultaneously, touched an important thread: how do we deal with two different media on the same subject, simultaneously? Perhaps it is not too difficult.

> *Nothing is less real than realism. Details are confusing – It is only by selection, by elimination, by emphasis . . . that we get at the real meaning of things.*[9]

Bachelard says:

> *The man with the magnifying glass – bars the every-day world. He is a fresh eye before a new object. The botanist's magnifying glass is youth recaptured. It gives him back the enlarging gaze of a child. With this glorious glass in hand, he returns to the garden.*[10]

> *It is surprising to me to see how many people separate the objective from the abstract. . . . The abstraction is often the most definite form of the intangible thing in myself that I can only clarify in paint.*[11]

How can we understand terms like 'abstraction', 'realism', 'objective' or even 'spiritual'? Part of the problem is that every art, every academic discipline has its own vocabulary. O'Keeffe is a perfect example of clarity of thought from her perspective, but illusive in unified clarification of her art on the part of others. She was continually attempting to clarify the interpretations of critics of her works, which often dramatically differed from her own – particularly in the area of sexuality in her works in general, and flowers in particular.

A different type of illusive language is seen in the Bachelard quote. Yes, we see various aspects of the gaze, but the creative artist transfers the vision back to an audience, by means of an artefact that transfers the vision. The artefact demonstrates what was experienced by the creator, often including how that creator actually felt, emotionally, about the experience. For example, the conclusion of Mahler's *Symphony No. 9* leaves little doubt about the composer's feelings about his impending death, and his sorrow over his broken marriage. It is not difficult; it merely requires honesty, and the ability to touch that part of oneself. Words, alone, do not transfer feeling, unless transference is in the intent.

Consider several examples by Cather and Lawrence. They are writing about landscapes, and the mountains are geographically close to those painted by O'Keeffe. Several authors use scenic descriptions to strengthen the drama of the narrative. Willa Cather (*Death Comes for the Archbishop*, 1927) and D.H. Lawrence (*St. Mawr*, 1924) wrote about the mountains and landscapes that were geographically close to the paintings of those same subjects . . . close to the same time she was actually painting there.

★

From several points of view, we find several descriptions of mountains and one of the prairie grasslands of Nebraska. Descriptive words are successful in that they place the reader into the setting, so that they feel present by reacting to the sights. Words transfer the reader from their reading chair to, into, the landscape if the writer succeeds in the power of their descriptive language. When the reader (audience) participates in the transfer from words on pages to feeling a part of the actual scene, the creative process involving the unfolding of X is working.

We note that words are always part of a moving construct; they appear, and are remembered, in time. Each word or line in a poem is something that unfolds – meaning changes with each addition. There is no present: only past and future exist. As we read the landscape descriptions, our imagination changes with each additional noun, and nouns are modified in their meaning by each additional adjective. Information is constantly subject to revision in arts that occur in time. A painting, a novel or a photograph are present in their entirety upon the first contact with them. (Yes, there is a temporal element in the passage of the eye over a visual artefact or the speed of the eye as it peruses pages of words.)

But the visual art, a painting, is totally present, with obvious boundaries. But it is a different type of transfer of emotion from the reader of words; the former is under the control of the painter, the latter under the control of the reader. Participation is different; words have meaning in context, while paintings and photographs are the context. For the latter, time is frozen. Let us probe a little more deeply into this issue, as we are entering a new domain.

Words about mountains and the prairie activate the visual memory imagination. Paintings about these same contents present an already-formed imaginative picture. We are considering different contexts. The psyche already has contextual associations; it merely depends on how these associations are activated that determines the level of feeling or emotion in the viewer/reader's responses.

The context has touched some part of the reader/viewer – a historic moment, an archetype, a complex that is brought to consciousness. Only the stimuli are presented to the psyche; reality works itself out. Words are hints; the boundaries of the visual art are a means of confirming what the viewer can make of the information.

Each art enters the unconscious in a different way. The question I wish to now pose is this: how are we to understand paintings and words that are about the same subject, created at the same time in roughly the same locale?

⋆

Georgia O'Keeffe's first experience with the vitality of the land was in Texas, where she taught for several years (1912–14, 1916–18).

> *On the plains of the Panhandle, distance, space, and isolation were abundant, noise, crowds, and visual obstructions few.*[12]

> *(Like Amarillo) . . . the wind blows like mad – and there is nothing after the last house of town as far as you can see – there is something wonderful about the bigness and the loneliness and the windiness of it all.*[13]

The vastness of the landscape obviously had a profound impact upon her. One can imagine standing where, as far as the eye can see, there is nothing. It is not difficult to sense the effect this had on someone of O'Keeffe's temperament: surrounded on all sides by the emptiness. The focus begins to stop swirling and settles upon the solitary figure of . . . the artist who can make artistic use of the moment. She is truly isolated: a state of mind – an epiphany in the making – a dangerous point in the psyche where the entire life narrative is simultaneously focusing on the artist and being coaxed into the unconscious.

Solitary . . . lonely . . . alone . . . outside

Comparing O'Keeffe's isolation with that of Kahlo, we find ourselves in a rather puzzling situation. They actually met on several occasions. Outwardly the women were quite similar. Both were politically involved, in many of the same causes. They were both married to men who were continually sexually involved with other women . . . a state of infidelity also pursued by Frida and Georgia. This was the era of the sexual revolution. Frida was always surrounded by friends, active in politics and frequently at gatherings of the current group of Mexican artists of all genres. But her paintings, which are largely self-portraits, are her autobiography.

O'Keeffe's isolation is more a function of place; she enjoyed solitude, and yet her paintings (seemingly) contain little of her personal narrative, and are almost totally without people.

O'Keeffe disguised her anguish and isolation from the outside world, as best she could. As stated, her marriage to the photographer was often disastrous. In their beginning together, they were a professional couple who were seemingly okay. (Refer to *Between the Sheets*[14] for discussions of writers' marriages to each other).

Alfred Stieglitz was a distinguished photographer, gallery owner and a prominent voice in the promotion of American art and artists. He was O'Keeffe's mentor and early promoter of her work, which he remained throughout his life. He often photographed O'Keeffe, focusing largely on her hands, and on her nude body. He displayed the nude photos early in their relationship, leading to a lifelong difficulty for O'Keeffe.

Her sexuality became a prominent topic in reviews, especially when describing the flowers. Stieglitz benefited greatly from the sexualization of his model and wife; she never was pleased with his promotion of her erotic photos and the sexual content that he found in her work. She denied that aspect of herself throughout their life, but she never made him desist from this manner of aiding her career – including her income. All of her life she denied the depiction of female genitalia associated with her flowers. However, what others saw was not what she said she painted . . . at least consciously.

Frida Kahlo controlled her pain-ridden life by painting self-portraits. The colours she used were similar to the pastel building that one sees in her home in Coyoacan, and of the rich flora so plentiful in this tropical-like country. She sought to live, speak and paint freely – to overcome the patriarchy and Catholicism that controlled much of Mexican culture and thought in the early days of the twentieth century. She was a Marxist, a feminist, a sexually promiscuous artist, a product of the liberal part of Mexican culture that recognized its pre-Columbian and mythological history. For both O'Keeffe and Kahlo, the cultures of the native Indians were important – in their art and in their lives.

Kahlo's father was a photographer, and much of her portraiture resembles professional photographs. O'Keeffe was even more influenced by photography, especially that of Stieglitz, Paul Strand and Ansel Adams. Some of her paintings show a close resemblance to works of these three.

Eventually, O'Keeffe could no longer live with Stieglitz's womanizing. By the later 1920s, she had surpassed him in fame and income. The respective roles they had played – the personas they had created – were no longer viable. After several nervous breakdowns, O'Keeffe left the marriage. Kahlo had also divorced Rivera, but returned to the (re)marriage, and lived out an asexual life with him. So much of these two marriages is similar to that of Scott and Zelda Fitzgerald.

⋆

Stieglitz had made no attempt to keep his many extra-marital relationships private. O'Keeffe seemingly did know all about them since Stieglitz almost put them on display. Eventually, O'Keeffe confronted him, which she had never done in the past. She had internalized his behaviour and permitted herself extreme stress. This was part of her mental narrative throughout most of her life. Her compensatory behaviour was isolation, introversion . . . and art. Kahlo's compensatory behaviour was quite opposite: boundless energy, extraversion . . . and art. Kahlo's psyche was perfectly articulated in her paintings; they were about her and her suffering. But in spite of her personal statements regarding her artistic intentions, it is necessary to probe more deeply into the unconscious symbols that O'Keeffe continually projected. She appeared to find solace in her isolation, if we view that part of her paintings in this way.

★

The flowers represent something very different for many of those who view them. They are, as O'Keeffe says, only flowers. And yet, when compared to clinical illustrations, they are quite similar to female genitalia. Lewis Mumford suggested that her work was highly erotic:

> *she has concentrated and celebrated almost every phase of the erotic experience. . . . The Pictures are not derivations, they are sources.*[15]

It is the work of the viewer to judge as to the eroticism in the paintings. Given her constant denial, coupled with her obvious erotic aura, it is a legitimate question to inquire about the unconscious projections in her flowers, landscapes and bones works.

O'Keeffe, like Kahlo, did not confine herself to one partner in her sexual adventures. Although not as overt as Kahlo, or Rivera and Stieglitz for that matter, she was physically and emotionally desirous of a vigorous sexual life. To a lover from her days in Texas, she wrote:

> *If you knew how very much afraid I am to say and do things sometimes you would think my nerve in doing them inexcusable.*[16]
>
> *I wondered if you had done what I wanted you to last night . . . I suppose you did but I can't remember whom or where or how. Maybe I did it.*[17]

Kahlo's sexual life, as a result of her place in Mexico's artistic culture – she was a celebrity – was more public than O'Keeffe's. She once told her biographer (Herrera) that her very strong sexual needs led her to a view of life: 'Make love, take a bath, make love again.'[18]

Aside from powerful libidos, both women shared a love for flowers. We know about O'Keeffe's; as for Kahlo: 'I paint flowers so they will not die.'[19] Although it is somewhat difficult to authenticate this quote, Kahlo's feelings for flowers is borne out by an examination of many of her portraits; in many of them, she is wearing flowers in her hair. There are also flowers in the patterns on the wall, and in her dresses. The backgrounds often contain Mexican fauna, including leaves and vines – sometimes all at the same time – and sometimes including monkeys or dogs. But it is different to view a picture whose entire canvas deals with a photographic, close-up view of one flower. It is somehow easier to see flowers as ornamentation.

Enlargement and focus upon one object increases attention; there is no other place to look, except away. It seems as though it would take more energy to focus on background or on ornamentation, for they are the aspects of the painting that bring focus onto the foreground; they are also that part of orchestration which necessitates both simultaneously playing and staying out of the way of a soloist in a concerto performance. Both Kahlo and O'Keeffe use flowers frequently. But for neither are they the entire story, but rather a thread that must be followed.

★

Four creators, two painters and two novelists began this voyage of discovery with the simple focus on mountains. If my intuition is correct, and if there is some part of X in all four, it is necessary to re-examine our information with a more probing focus. To do this, we must return to the large room in the Gallery of the Soul, where creative artists are exploring that which is there to become known – their own unconscious psyches – which we are continuing to illuminate. This pathway will be useful only if it presents questions raised by the actual works of art, rather than some part of the narratives that must be superficially imposed. If we move further into the unconscious of the creative artists I have been discussing, beyond the paintings and words, we find something that substantively links the four to their works, it will further our discussion.

For example: Both the subjects of the novels created, and the painters, share a vision of the woman as outsider.

In the marriages of Kahlo and O'Keeffe, both women were in similarly intolerable positions; both were strong, independent and brilliantly creative painters who found themselves in open marriages in which they seem to have been unwilling participants. While neither of the women was sexually monogamous, they appeared to be far more wounded by what was occurring. (It may even be that the sexual affairs of the women were in response to those of their husbands – but this is only conjecture.) What is certain is that these two women were outsiders in, and victims of, patriarchal societies that placed women in positions inferior to those of men.

This is the position of the women in the D.H. Lawrence novels of this time (*The Woman Who Rode Away*, *St. Mawr*, *The Princess* – all directly written in and about Lawrence's time in Taos, and the follow-up *The Virgin and the Gypsy*) and place; it is also consistent with the heroine of Cather's *My Antonia*. The women characters in the novels and Frida Kahlo lead into a more sociological pathway that I wish to pursue. This chapter began with, and is mainly concerned with, Georgia O'Keeffe.

Art historian Anna Chave has written an exciting and provocative article: 'O'Keeffe and the Masculine Gaze'.[20] Conceptually guided by Freudian/Lacanian psychoanalysis, it suggests new pathways in our discussion of sexuality. In particular, it opens the issue of desire, which, in turn, reopens some of the most basic material thus far presented in a manner that I have been pursuing throughout this study. While O'Keeffe's colours attracted attention, the shapes of the mountains only seemed to attract notice.

(Lacan is difficult to understand. I suggest that the reader consult the References at the end of this chapter for greater details on Lacan's theories.)[21,22]

★

In a review of an O'Keeffe retrospective in 1988, Brenson referred to her 'almost mystical feeling for the unions of the human body with the body of the natural world'.[23] How interesting that, even in a generally negative review, the critic would note the 'mystical feeling' of the painter.

'Mystical feeling' means that something quite definitive and quite powerful has been communicated to the viewer. And, what is the 'body' of which he writes? In what way(s) is it united with the natural world? The words quoted, and the questions asked about them, suggest that something new has appeared, even if it is an extension of an earlier idea; something remains unexamined.

O'Keeffe herself spoke about the difficulty of words:

> *I found that I could say things with colors and shapes that I couldn't say in any other way – things that I had no words for.*[24]

In O'Keeffe's mind, there is validity to a feeling projected by a painting . . . another way of citing her desire to make known the unknown. To do so, she had to pioneer a new concept:

> *What distinguishes Miss O'Keeffe is the fact that she has discovered a beautiful language . . . and has created in this language a new set of symbols; by means of these she has opened up a whole area of human consciousness.*[25]

Opening an area of human consciousness generally belongs within the field of psychoanalysis, but reading any Greek comedy or tragedy dispels that idea. (I need go no further than the name Oedipus.) But it is also true that, during the period we are discussing, the first few decades of the twentieth century, Freud and Jung were much discussed. But the issue raised in this discussion, the place of women in patriarchal society, had been prevalent for a far longer period of time – certainly as far back as the early nineteenth century – and has been thematically in the forefront of great literature ever since. But it seems that much of this literature has addressed the psychologically conscious elements of the patriarchy, not pursuing consciousness deeply enough, or daringly enough, to reach through the immediate personal narratives into the collective associations necessary for a more compelling understanding of the individual psyche.

The unconscious issue that is being addressed is the sexuality of the female body: consciously addressed by Chave, unconsciously in the work of O'Keeffe. From another viewpoint, Chave addresses the same exhibition that Brenson reviewed:

> *What the recent O'Keeffe retrospective offered the public was something rather exceptional: a woman's often vivid, poetic and evocative report on her own experience of her body and her desires.*[26]

The pathway to desire was often spoken about in earlier times, but usually as a feeling that the subject had for the object: what I want, from you. In opening 'desire' from the unconscious wrapping in which it is usually contained, we find a thought of a flexible feeling that is transferable . . . in both directions. It is reciprocity of feeling.

We now open what has become a new pathway; desire for the creative arts is an integral part of the journey to and from X, in Chapter 1. A work of art is a projection, the attraction to that work a magnet. Desire is omnidirectional. Art does not speak to only one person . . . it is the product of one person's touching that deeply unconscious part of the psyche . . . the archetype. And since the archetypes are manifestations of the collective, they too are shared. We are discussing needs and demands, with desire being somewhere linguistically between these two. Desire cycles between individuals and/or entire cultures. If we take one additional step into the unconscious, we realize that we are basically dealing with the feeling function, discussed earlier in Chapter 3.

O'Keeffe was able to project desire, from her unconscious; in this case, she 'spoke' about sexual desire, the most intimate connection we have with another human being. It appears that she never had a relationship in which she enjoyed such intimacy, except in her paintings:

> *The parts of the body she engaged were mainly without interior*[27] *. . . a model of sexuality and sexual development centered around voids (vaginas, wombs) and penetrability, rather than the probing penis . . .*[28] *as it describes abstractly, what differentiates female bodies: the roundness, the flows and, above all, the spaces.*[29] *She has levelled the intricacies of love's juncture with the purity and the absence of share that lovers feel in this meeting . . . she has, in sum, found a language to experiences that are too intimate to be shared.*[30]

The four women of Lawrence's novels are attempting to find themselves within the sexually dysfunctional patriarchy. They were all women who needed to break away from their environment. None ultimately succeeded in the sense that Connie Chatterley did. But none had the strength of the latter. Perhaps, in one way or another, the four others were studies for Lady Chatterley. But probably none of the others projected desire as did Connie.

From all the jagged, masculine mountains of Lawrence and Cather, smoothed out by millennia of flowing waters that O'Keeffe must have experienced in studying the shapes of these same mountains, there was a projection of desire. And within the terrain of the softly rolling plains of the Nebraska farmland, the lovely Antonia lived a life following the template under which she grew and matured – a pioneer woman – with ten children and an unbroken spirit. Each spoke in a language familiar to them; O'Keeffe's was invented, Cather's seemed traditional. Both spoke in the language of a new country . . . their new country.

Kahlo also spoke her own language. The difference is that her desire was for you to see her. She was the creature of the mirror; she must be in control both of what she projects and what the viewer absorbs.

O'Keeffe projected herself through carefully, and probably unconsciously, designed symbols. She touched the archetype, and opened a door for the viewer to walk through, and also reach to touch, and be touched.

References

1 Asensio, P. *Frank Lloyds Wright, Georgia O'Keeffe*. New York: HarperCollins, 2003, p. 41.
2 Eliot, T.S. *Four Quartets*, New York: Harcourt Brace & Company, p. 13.
3 Buhler, L. *et al.* 'Black Mesa Landscape'. In *Georgia O'Keeffe and New Mexico: A Sense of Place*. Princeton, NJ: Princeton University Press, 2004, pp. 14–15.
4 Ibid. 'The Cliff Chimneys', pp. 24–25.
5 Kotz, M.L. 'A day with Georgia O'Keeffe'. *Art News*, December 1977. Quoted in Eisler, B. *O'Keeffe and Stieglitz*. New York: Penguin, 1991, p. 327.
6 Asensio, p. 53.
7 Kandinsky, W. *Concerning the Spiritual in Art*. New York: Dover, 1977, p. 10.
8 Ibid., p. 10.
9 O'Keeffe, G. *Some Memories of Drawing*. New York: Viking, 1976.
10 Bachelard, G. *The Poetry of Space*. M. Jolas (trans). Boston, MA: Beacon Press, 1994, p. 155.
11 O'Keeffe, 1976.
12 Udall, S. *O'Keeffe and Texas*. San Antonio, TX: McNay Art Museum, 1998, p. 15.
13 Ibid.
14 McDowell, L. *Between the Sheets*. New York: Overlook, 2010.
15 Mumford, L. 'The art galleries, sacred and profane'. *New Yorker,* 10 February 1934, p. 403. Quoted in Robinson, R. *Georgia O'Keeffe*: A *Life*. Lebanon, NH: University Press of New England, 1989, p. 403.
16 Robinson, R. and O'Keeffe, G. *A Life*. Hanover, NE: University Press of New England, 1989, p. 114.
17 Eisler, B. O'Keeffe, G. and Steiglitz, A. *An American Romance*. New York: Penguin Books, 1991, p. 77.
18 Herrera, H. *Frida*. New York: Harper & Row, 1983, p. 199.

19 Kennedy, R. '"Frida Kahlo's garden" to sprout in New York City'. *New York Times*, 13 June 2014, Arts Beat, p. C3.
20 Chave, A. 'O'Keeffe and the masculine gaze'. *Art in America*, January 1990, p. 115.
21 Lacan, J. *Feminine Sexuality*. J. Rose (trans). New York: Pantheon, 1982.
22 www.lacanonline.com. 'What does Lacan say about . . . desire', 9 May 2010.
23 Brenson, M. 'How O'Keeffe painted hymns to god and spirit'. *New York Times*, 18 November 1987, *Art View*.
24 Stieglitz, A. 'A. Stieglitz Presents'. New York: Anderson Galleries, 1923.
25 McBride, H. 'Modern art'. *Dial*, May 1926, p. 437.
26 Chave, p. 116.
27 Ibid.
28 Irigary, L. *Speculum of the Other Woman*, G. Gill (trans). Ithaca, NY: Cornell University Press, 1985, p. 22.
29 Chave, 'O'Keeffe and the masculine gaze'.
30 Mumford, L. 'O'Keefe(sic) and Matisse'. O'Keeffe Exhibit. New York: Intimate Gallery, 1928, p. 42.

13
MUSIC IN FILM

Audiences are captive to what appears on screen during movies, and even more so to the music that is used in films. There is no choice; either the music works with the dialogue and scenic design, or it does not. The viewer who is generally in a state of consciousness assimilates the accompanying musical soundtrack. It works. The music has to be terrible for the audience to reject it, or the entire movie because of it; but the composers who work on films are generally very good.

However, a question arises when the music is already well known, but in a different context. If the film is not directly about the music being used, but that music is identified in a different context by the audience, what is to be gained … and by whom?

The three films I will discuss are *Death in Venice* (Visconti, 1971),[1] *Ludwig* (Visconti, 1972)[2] and *Melancholia* (von Trier, 2011).[3] Mahler's 'Adagietto' from his *Symphony No.5* is used in *Death in Venice*, and Wagner's *Prelude to Tristan and Isolde* is used in the other two. In all three films, the music is used for its affect. In an Ingmar Bergman film the music is so much a part of the narrative that it is noticeable but not intrusive. In the films under discussion, the music is generally intrusive; it tends to aid in telling the story rather than underlying some particular event. In *Death in Venice* and *Melancholia*, the directors have successfully used the music, but not so in *Ludwig*. The success or failure of using music that is widely known in another context, rests upon the director's full understanding of both the affective and structural nature of the music with which they are working. If one is listening too carefully to the music, it gets in the way. It is commentary in the background, not affect enhancing in the foreground.

⋆

There is very little music in the repertoire that is as powerful and communicative as the 'adagietto' of Mahler's *Symphony No. 5*. It holds audiences in its grasp like no other. It is sometimes difficult to breathe during a performance, not wanting to disturb yourself or others with the noise. This is the movement of the piece that Visconti chose for his movie on *Death in Venice*.

This is a story of unrequited love, between an ageing composer, Gustav von Aschenbach, and a beautiful pre-teen Polish boy, Tadzio. The composer and the boy's family are vacationing in Venice, with death from an outbreak of cholera lurking in the immediate future. The drama is furthered almost exclusively by the music. The film begins with the composer's boat approaching Venice, shrouded in darkness. The scene presents the film's credits, and the only complete hearing of the symphony's movement. The only other lengthy hearing is at the very end, with a final view of the young boy surrounded by shimmering light, and the composer quietly dying in his chair on the beach. Both are alone, isolated from their environments. The film's closing credits appear as the death scene fades into darkness.

The book's storyline is, in itself, extremely powerful – the narrative of an old, successful composer reaching the end of his life, his career, yet obsessed with a young boy who merely toys with him. There are flashbacks of various parts of his life, including the death of a daughter. He is perpetually monitoring his appearance; during his death scene, a thin line of hair dye is running down his face. So many things that occurred in the composer's life were, perhaps, taken from the life of Mahler.

The music occurs in situations where Visconti wants to mark something of importance, but it is always an excerpt, without continuity. It is as if the music is briefly acknowledging the event, and quickly moving on. It always works, because of the nature of the music itself. The melody and harmony exist in this constant tension, where non-harmonic notes appear on the strong part of the beat and are resolved on the weak part. The listener is constantly waiting for the resolution of dissonance, which, due to the nature of expectation, gives the music the feeling of forward motion. (Wagner uses the same musical language in *Tristan and Isolde*.) It is fascinating that Wagner's music is an idea for the end of the world, as depicted in *Melancholia*, but would not be appropriate for the quiet, contemplative . . . ultimate sadness of Gustav von Aschenbach's death. That setting needed Mahler.

Ludwig is the story of the relationship between the 'mad king' and Wagner, whose monumental narcissism and arrogance were the perfect complement to Ludwig's insanity. As in *Death in Venice*, the costumes and settings of *Ludwig* are masterful. The obsession in this film is Ludwig's for Wagner, although in this case it is probably not sexual. Ludwig's homosexuality was very obvious to all; he had an entire coterie of gay friends, and there is a gay orgy scene near the end of the film that serves as the final affirmation of Ludwig's near total disintegration.

Homosexuality was the ultimate sin of his day; blended with constant pressure on Ludwig to marry, he needed to continually find funds to support Wagner's lifestyle. Ludwig went from being rather odd at the film's beginning to completely insane at the end. Ultimately, he killed himself. At the end of this film, with Ludwig lying dead in the rain, and as the credits begin to roll, Visconti uses a Wagner piano piece that was played throughout the film. The piece utilizes the same harmonic gestures as the Tristan work and is consistently repeated throughout the film. Some music simply does not bear repetition, particularly music of such questionable quality.

The true villain of this story is Wagner. His incessant demands upon Ludwig were beyond extraordinary. Ludwig's patronage was unlimited but, ultimately, the state treasury was not. His manipulation of Ludwig was a perfect fit for Wagner. They were very much a co-dependent couple.

The use of music in this film is like that in *Death in Venice*. Music is used to highlight certain scenes, and is built upon its affective nature – the power to influence through sound alone. In *Melancholia*, von Trier uses the same music, based upon its dramatic structure. Visconti seemed oblivious to the drama presented by Wagner's music. Part of its power is the continuity over a very long time; it is one continuous harmonic progression, the resolution coming with the last note in the opera – some three hours after its introduction. It is difficult to take small phrases out of the larger-than-life statement and expect them to relate in a continuous manner to the listener. It was easier in Visconti's use of Mahler, because that piece remained a dynamic entity; its rather short length and harmonic continuity mean that the structure can be maintained, and the interruptions for highlighting the meaning of Justine can be kept intact.

But as we move into a discussion of *Melancholia*, using the same work by Wagner, we find a greater understanding of what the music, and his own film, are about. It feels as though the director of the first two films, sometimes like the conductor of an orchestra, allowed the music to be in control and simultaneously out of control. Artistic events should flow naturally, and if they do not there should be some explanation for why that is the case. In *Ludwig*, the expectations built up by the musical expectations of the piece, and the attendant need for more musical information, are secondary to the need for some kind of personal gratification by Visconti. He had done such a magnificent job with Mahler, but of course he had better music with which to work.

Melancholia presents another set of circumstances. It contains a variety of transformational incidents – successes and failures. The drama is nuanced, as is this linkage to Wagner. It is a text rich with nuance, an end-of-the-world scenario. This film is actually not about the end of *the* world; rather, it is an end of someone's world. There are a number of characters to whom this would apply; in fact, only the little boy, Leo, and Justine, his aunt, have no need for the world to end.

All of the characters, with these two as exceptions, exhibit powerful obsessive behaviours, but Justine bears the stigma of being 'mentally ill'. I doubt there are many individuals who could bear such treatment from others and have any equanimity about themselves. When one finds a person who is a veritable pincushion at the service of her family – and possibly extended family too – it is difficult to understand, in reality, the actions of the other characters. 'Sadism' is a word that would clearly describe the situation, but pre-transformational would be better.

As the film begins with her wedding, caution should be observed in placing the mentally ill person in situations from which it is difficult for her to emerge. Such was her wedding, complete with ghastly dinner speeches and an inability to have sex with her new husband. The situation is not sustainable; something must occur.

★

Tristan and Isolde is an opera with constantly moving tension that moves towards disaster. It is a medieval romance filled with tragedy, finally ending in death for the lovers. It is the type of story that could have been expected by the creator of the *Ring Cycle* and *Die Meistersinger*. The weaknesses of Wagner's texts and the disdain for his personal and political life are one aspect of the man; the other side is a group of fantastic operas, musically. *Tristan* is his crowning musical achievement.

The reason for venturing into this music is not derived from the ego position of Lars von Trier; rather, it is to confront the existential realities of the contemporary world on a planet-wise basis. This music, with its unidirectional movement, which is constantly building tension, is consistent with the director's vision.

Built from a small example – a family wedding – von Trier gradually widens the lens through which he is viewing behaviours, not to include more characters, but to increase the strength of the focus on the original people. This is, conceptually, what he received from the flow of Wagner's music.

The lens widens for the exposition of the characters. They are: Justine, the bride; Justine's sister Claire and her husband Michael, their little boy Leo; Justine's husband-to-be Michael; her parents; and her boss, Jack. The screenplay follows the traditional format of standard drama: characters are introduced and assemble; something is learned about each of the characters; something disastrous happens.

We begin by noticing that the bride, Justine, seems confused and ultimately realize that she's dissociating at her own wedding. The trauma, seemingly felt only by Justine, occurs when her parents offer their wedding toasts: disgusting taunting of each other. This provides the beginning of a psychic shock that is a harbinger of what is to come. The dissociation spreads throughout the guests, accompanied by the appearance of a period in which all are in liminal space – a point from which transformation is possible. The danger, metaphorical or real, which is present and constantly moving towards the assembled guests, is another planet, named Melancholia, on course to smash into earth.

As the drama unfolds, each character battles the risk of ego loss, the dismissal of denial, against which fear and insecurity remain. Transformation and submission to the vulnerability of exploring the unconscious is a difficult concept to accept; living with the fear of change is, for many, easier than accepting responsibility for one's inner being.

Details emerge about the nature of each of the characters. Where Justine is involved, the music returns in excerpts, the entire prelude never being used. As each character exposes points of extreme vulnerability, Melancholia (the planet named after a mental condition) moves closer. There is a desperate need for Claire and John to embrace the reality of the world, particularly Justine's. She has been aware of the approaching Melancholia the entire time, and has accepted its presence. The other characters in the film have all left, self-righteously choking on their own denial. John resolves his scientific failure – he predicted that the Melancholia would never strike earth – by committing suicide. Justine, Claire and the ever-innocent Leo remain to encounter Melancholia at the film's conclusion.

The ending brings in Wagner's music (von Trier has been using only the prelude in the film), from its beginning to the most powerful section, a section that coincides with the planet actually striking the earth. The screen goes blank. There is silence as the credits roll.

*

Justine was 'mentally ill'. Her disorder could be classified as melancholia, a physical illness with a psychological origin. It may leave the patient incapacitated for a time or helpless, unable to deal with a constant onslaught from others.

Justine was certainly under constant siege, to varying degrees, from all of the characters in the wedding party – except Leo. But she gradually succeeded in transforming herself by no longer allowing her ego to accept what was being projected on to her. This transformation is depicted in a fantastic pictorial montage, somewhat akin to the one used by Bergman in *Persona.*

Justine understands the reality of melancholia. She realizes that none of it is real, and that she is capable of being free. Claire, however, remains fearful. And Leo is peacefully following the pathway offered by Justine.

In the opera, Isolde sings a heart-rending aria at the very conclusion. It would not have been appropriate to use in the film, because *Melancholia* is not a love story. But certainly, the sorrow felt, the feeling in the audience of having been touched in a very meaningful way – and transformed by the experience – maybe this was why von Trier did not use Isolde's final 'love death' aria, and ended the story at the point of oblivion.

Transformation would mean that those encountering *Melancholia* would take the experience and begin to ask the same questions of themselves that von Trier posed to the characters in his film. This is what art is all about.

References

1 Visconti, L. (Dir.). *Death in Venice.* Warner Brothers, 1971.
2 Visconti, L. (Dir.). *Ludwig.* Mega Film Roma, 1972.
3 Trier, L. von (Dir.) *Melancholia.* Magnolia Home Entertainment, 2012.

14

THE PIANO

It is difficult to discuss *The Piano*[1] from a unified perspective, as if it were the restructuring of a particular myth or the dramatization of a particular symptom. While the characters do, in fact, exemplify some basic concepts of depth psychology, the presence of one particular character, the piano, places all others in a unique position.

Although it acts as neither filter nor censor, the piano is the generating force of all that occurs. It moves the action, both physical and emotional. It is a causal force, ever present as foreground or background via the music that flows from it.

In the foreground, it is a physical presence that is literally moved several times, adding impact to the tensions of the narrative; the shifting of locations is an aspect of the tension of opposites, symbolic of the need for control. In the background, it represents the spirited presence of the empowerment it provides to the main character in the film. But it also serves as the catalyst for the competition between the two male characters for the attention of the female.

The narrative is uncomplicated. There are four characters: Ada, a mute woman who has been betrothed to a New Zealand landowner; Flora, Ada's 10-year-old daughter; Stewart, a resident New Zealander to whom Ada has been promised with no discernible agreement on her part; and Baines, another New Zealander, and neighbour of Stewart. There are additional subsidiary characters: groups of English settlers and New Zealand Maoris, both of which function as Greek choruses.

Aside from the brief opening and closing scenes that accompany monologues with the voice of Ada, the narrative begins and ends in the sea, on the New Zealand coast. The filmmaker, Jane Campion, has used marvellous landscapes brilliantly. The land of New Zealand functions as a beautiful hint of Romanticism, but also as a warning of isolation and alienation. The journey occurs in two stages, which ultimately becomes one of individuation. The first is Ada's crossing the Atlantic to New Zealand. The second is from there: the trek to and from Stewart's home, and from there to and from Baines' home, represents Ada's journey. Although the geographic distance is short, the psychic gulf that she bridges is immense. Her sacrifice at the end demonstrates the distance she has traversed. She has been ruptured from her home in England. The drama of the film occurs in liminal space, the space of floating through a web of nothingness, struggling with external forces over which she has no control: marriage to an unacceptable stranger, and estrangement from her piano – her soul.

Ada and Flora arrive in a boat with their goods and Ada's piano. Everything is unloaded onto a deserted beach, awaiting Stewart's arrival. While waiting, we are drawn into Campion's images of isolation and abandonment.[2] These feelings of isolation are beautifully articulated by the camera. (It is interesting to note that the creator who uses a camera manages to absorb the instrument as part of their psyche. We have experienced this in *Clea* and will do so again in this film.) Stewart arrives a day late, with some Maori helpers and his neighbour, Baines.

Stewart has all of the goods taken by Maori workers, except for the cumbersome piano, a powerful rupture for Ada, not one caused by geography. It burns deeply into Ada's psyche. Upon arriving at Stewart's home, Ada and Stewart pose for wedding pictures amidst a driving rain; afterwards, Ada rips off her wedding dress in disgust, tearing it. During the next few scenes, Stewart leaves on a trip and Ada persuades Baines to take her back to the beach. Once there she begins to play the piano, even though it is still in its crate. Her entire demeanour changes: she smiles and weaves with the music, while Flora dances. Upon experiencing these reactions, Baines begins to transcend his own ego boundary, opening towards Ada. He has been visited, emotionally, by a muse, and begins to compensate for her losses.

At Stewart's house, Ada carves piano keys into the kitchen table; Stewart labels her behaviour 'abnormal'. The lives of Ada, Stewart and Baines interweave around the piano, culminating in a trade: Baines offers Stewart 80 acres of land for the piano. Baines has the piano reconditioned, eventually making a deal with Ada whereby she can earn back her piano, one key per visit, by playing for him. But these are the keys to seduction, delivered by Eros. Eventually Baines and Ada convert the energy communicated by the piano to sexual energy . . . and embarrassed socializing . . . to love.

Stewart learns of their affair from Flora, and ends it first by barricading Ada and Flora in their house, and then by chopping off one of Ada's fingers in retaliation, because of her continuing love affair with Baines. This scene, with its brutality and Ada's stare of defiance from a pool of mud, ends Ada's journey, and serves as the film's climax. The impasse ends with Stewart allowing Ada and Flora to leave with Baines. As they leave from the same beach on which Ada and Flora had earlier landed, the piano is cast overboard as a safety measure, because of the instability of the overloaded boat. This is done at Ada's direction, and signals an important point of arrival in her journey. She almost drowns as the rope holding the piano pulls her into the sea; but she survives. The film ends with Ada teaching piano using a newly acquired prosthetic finger; she is also learning to speak.

The most interesting character in the film is Stewart, for it is he who obviously displays symptoms and projects his deeply troubled mental life on to Ada. He lives within a group of English colonists whose attempts to bring their homeland to this wilderness are often sadly humorous. Adjusting to their new home is not an option for them. And yet, they have experienced precisely the same kind of rupture as that experienced by Ada, except theirs was voluntary. Their response was to cling to their visions of the past; Ada's was to become mute.

Should the right conditions ensue, Stewart would be most likely to experience some sort of transformation. This from the perspective of depth psychology becomes more evident as the film continues. Baines' transformation is in keeping with his experiences – his narrative. His is a Romantic vision of relationships, and honesty. He is the opposite character, serving to give definition to this struggle for Ada; this competition strengthens the narrative, aligning the characters of Ada and Baines, and eventually Flora.

An issue of pathologizing unfolds in the following way: as Stewart approaches the beach for the first time, he pauses to comb his hair; and in the wedding photo scene, he removes his top hat to comb his hair, sparse as it is, then replaces the hat. In this futile gesture, we witness his insecurity. Given Stewart's complete power over Ada, this is odd behaviour. On first seeing her he responds to her mutism by observing that she seems small, wonders if she can hear him, and remarks that her growth is not what it should be.

The contrast between Stewart and Baines is established at this point, when Baines remarks that she appears to be tired, in response to Stewart. Stewart is manipulating Ada into the role of the identified patient by pathologizing her, in the Freudian sense: the symptom represents a certain lack, rather than a Jungian interpretation of a system out of balance. Later, when Stewart sees the piano keys carved into the table, he literalizes by saying that she is incapable of making sound. He also wonders if, in her mutism, her brain is affected, engaging in what Hillman terms 'nominal denial . . . for its focus is on the words, on the naming and classifying of psychic complaints'.[3]

Though Stewart is psychologizing Ada's 'symptoms' by cloaking them in pathology, thereby attempting to make the visible into a state of invisibility, he is also simultaneously demonstrating his own pathology:

> *The pathology is the place that keeps the person in the soul, that torment, that twist that you can't simply be naïve, you can't simply go along in a natural way, that there's something broken, twisted, hurting, that forces constant reflection – and work, in Bachelard's sense. There's a work going on all the time, a fire burning, there's something elemental happening.*[4]

It is this pathologizing that indicates Stewart's potential for transformation. Pathologizing is a powerful defence mechanism. It stigmatizes the recipient, or at least it attempts to do so. It is the person who is projecting the accusations with whom we should be concerned. We recognize the 'accuser' by the nature of the projections; the accusations as they rise from some unconscious need, appear quite similar – if not identical – to symptoms uncovered from verbal behaviour. These symptoms draw attention to a potential for transformation. In turn, the system produces an opportunity for change; in this case, change is to be brought about through individuation.

According to Williams:

> *Stewart has come face to face with a mystery beyond words. Ada has opened Stewart to his loneliness, to jealousy and rage, to sexuality, and finally to an uncanny compassion.*[5]

Stewart is the emotionally blocked colonialist, the exemplar of Christian capitalism, with its Augustinian notions of the superiority of man over nature and oppressive sexual mores. He is the one whose ego is at the centre of the universe but, as Williams points out, he is also the one who makes the ultimate sacrifice in giving up Ada, thus allowing her to leave with Baines. Within him, the story unfolds and resolves; without his symptoms there would be no drama.

★

The dramatic and psychological implications of the story allow us to see through the personal into the collective. Shared experiences are one thing; the experiences that penetrate beyond those lived by the various participants in the narrative yield greater meaning when juxtaposed with images and metaphors not directly present.

Stewart and Baines are immediately presented as archetypal opposites. While Stewart's image of Ada is of her symptoms, Baines sees her complete psyche – her soul. Stewart is the colonial empiricist, while Baines is natural man, the D.H. Lawrence Romantic. Stewart retains the manners and assumptions of the colonizer who speaks no Maori. Baines does speak the language, and blends in with them to the extent of tattooing his face. Neither of them 'understands' music; Stewart is too abstracted, but Baines understands emotion and feeling. Stewart wants to bargain with cheap goods for Maori land; Baines bargains with expensive property for Ada; he buys the piano from Stewart for 80 acres of land, succeeding in drawing her to his house, his body, his love.

These are Jungian opposites: (ego) consciousness (Stewart) versus the unconscious (Baines). This is illuminated by Jung's concept of the transcendent function:

> *Out of this collision of opposites the unconscious psyche always creates a third thing of an irrational nature, which the conscious mind neither expects nor understands. It presents itself in a form that is neither a straight 'yes' nor a straight 'no', and is consequently rejected by both. For the conscious mind knows nothing beyond the opposites and, as a result, has no knowledge of the thing that unites them. Since,*

> *however, the solution of the conflict through the union of opposites is of vital importance, and is moreover the very thing that the conscious mind is longing for, some inkling of the creative act, and of the significance of it, nevertheless gets through.*[6]

The 'third thing of an irrational nature' is, to the egos of both Stewart and Baines, the piano. However, attachment to the piano as property is ego-driven, hence rational. At this point, Stewart cannot differentiate the piano as object from Ada herself. And Ada, herself, is equated with music, an irrational activity. It is the music *per se* that Ada creates that is non-rational, from the unconscious – that which we are searching for.

It is this 'irrational' that seems to puzzle many who discuss the creative arts. There seems to be no room for discussion of something that is not bounded by rationality, or by their inability to understand it. I would guess that there is some fear of ignorance, or not being found to be intellectual enough. This becomes harmful to the discussions when the attitude develops its own form of pathologizing into linkages with the arts and either neurosis or madness. There is a rather large and articulate constituency among scientists and interdisciplinary scholars who focus on this issue. There are dozens of books that list some sort of art with some aspect of psychology. This is pathologizing with a vengeance. To make matters much worse, there are attempts to deal with music in the brain; the general problem here is that few, if any, of the experimenters have a clue regarding how music actually functions . . . which brings me back to Stewart.

Ada is mute, yet she speaks with her hands, in writing and in playing the piano. Ada's communication is an essential moving force in the drama. All action evolves from its absence and presence.

Flora, Ada's daughter, is an insignificant person in this drama. She carries messages between Ada and Baines, is the first to become aware of their lovemaking and is the one who alerts Stewart to their liaisons. The archetypal puella, the piano, is almost a substitute for the teddy bear or blanket: an object of security after the split from the mother, and yet functioning as a chain of attachment between the two. She remains a puella figure throughout. She also assumes the role of Hermes, the messenger, bringing news to Stewart of the affair between Ada and Baines.

Baines uses the piano to reach Ada's soul. He succeeds, unleashing Eros:

> *The growth of culture consists . . . in a progressive subjugation of the animal in man. . . . From time to time there passes as it were a wave of frenzy through the ranks of men too long constrained within the limitations of their culture. Antiquity experienced it in the Dionysian orgies . . .*[7]

As her unconscious arouses the long-lost soul, Ada is free to make her sacrifice. As the boat leaves the beach overloaded, it wobbles dangerously. Ada suggests that the piano be abandoned, in service to a higher good – the safety of her family.

Although the final symbol has her attached to the piano and drowning because of it, she herself slips loose and surfaces. There will be other pianos, and even other fingers; these are objects. What Ada has now is her soul.

Williams places the motivation for Stewart's sacrifice, in allowing Ada and Baines to leave, in the moment when Stewart finally 'hears' Ada – not her piano or its music, but her voice. This is as much as his process would allow at the time.

> *Only through their sacrifices do the characters resolve their internal conflicts and unexpectedly transcend their isolation.*[8]

Throughout, I have spoken about the power of the piano to create and motivate the action. The piano as object reality, dealt with by the ego. However, on a deeper level, it is the music that invisibly emanates from the piano that is actually penetrating the communication barriers and moving into the soul. The music reaches its audience through Baines.

The archetypal modes and scales that reach into us, are without the filtration of culture. They are groupings within the octave that have different orders of half and whole steps.

That part which reaches into us is not the modes and scales *per se*, but the groupings – both vertical (harmony) and horizontal (melody) – which are the organizing materials of music. Beethoven was superb at these parts of musical composition; by this, however, I do not mean to exclude his sense of rhythm and the dynamics of his orchestration. He was, simply, the best that had existed in music . . . along with Bach. He reached his audiences by bringing the archetypes into the concert hall.

Storr ties together the narrative and analytical aspects of *The Piano*:

> *Although music is not a belief system, I think that its importance and its appeal also depend upon its being a way of ordering human experience. Great music both arouses our emotions and also provides a framework within which our passions 'enjoy themselves', as Nietzsche put it. Music exalts life, enhances life, and gives it meaning . . . Music is a source of reconciliation, exhilaration, and hope which never fails.*[9]

'The hope which never fails' could have, as its symbolic representation, the music of *The Piano*.

References

1 Campion, J. (Dir.) *The Piano*. Australian Film Commission, 1993.
2 Williams, D. *The Piano: The Isolated, Constricted Self*. www.cgjungpage.org, 27 October 2013, p. 3.
3 Hillman, J. *Re-visioning Psychology*. New York: HarperCollins, 1975, p. 60.
4 Ibid., p. 140.
5 Williams, p. 8.

6 Jung, C. *Collected Works 9*, I, Para. 285.
7 Jung, C., *Collected Works* 7, Para. 17.
8 Williams, p. 8.
9 Storr, A. *Music and the Mind*. New York: Free Press, 1992, p. 188.

15

TIM WINTON'S *THE RIDERS*

Tim Winton's *The Riders* is a story of rupture and ensuing journeys of transformative healing. Like a medieval painting, the novel proceeds on several levels simultaneously: the narrative itself, the symbolic and the mythological.

The narrative begins with Fred Scully refurbishing a recently purchased cottage in Ireland. He, his wife Jennifer and daughter Billie had been in Europe for several years; on the spur of the moment, they decide to remain in Ireland. Billie and Jennifer return to their home in Australia to settle their affairs while Scully remains to make the new home habitable.

Two important events occur during this period. Scully discovers a tree in the middle of a road, with shards of cloth of varying ages tied to it. He later learns that it is called the 'wishing tree'. And, one evening he awakes to see lights at the deserted castle near his cottage. Upon investigation, he also hears sounds from a procession of horsemen. They are dressed in medieval attire, with mud and blood smeared all over them. They are armed, wild-haired, cloaked and high booted. They smell bad and their horses are wild-eyed and snorting. Scully attempts to talk to the riders, but there is no response. Fearful, he leaves.

With the help of an Irish friend, Peter, Scully completes the work. He receives several telegrams informing him of progress in Australia. Scully arrives at the airport to meet Jennifer and his daughter; Billie gets off the plane, alone. The rupture has occurred.

Billie cannot speak, a victim of selective mutism. Scully cannot get any information regarding Jennifer's whereabouts, and alternates between states of understandable panic and total lack of comprehension. Following some vague clues, he attempts to find Jennifer by revisiting those places where the family had lived during their stay in Europe. This is the beginning of Scully's and to a lesser extent Billie's journey of transformation.

First, they travel to the Greek island where Jennifer had studied painting, while Scully worked and Billie attended school. Jennifer's former mentor Alex informs Scully that his student had no talent but beautiful legs. Alex is one of the confusing group of 'friends' with whom Scully and Jennifer interacted during their European stay. He is a finely etched, totally decadent character.

Scully, at the beginning of his journey in search of Jennifer, is suspicious of many of their former friends – could they be shielding Jennifer? He searches Alex's home and questions him until satisfied that she is not, nor has ever been, there. They relax into a more convivial discussion.

Alex is profoundly depressed, and commits suicide the next day. Scully is afraid of getting involved in an investigation, so he and Billie flee, having found no trace of Jennifer. Billie is bitten by a mad dog, and Scully acts as her doctor. Billie finally breaks her silence by shouting at him to stop. This is in response to Scully's doctoring, or perhaps it is an existential cry. The two then take a dangerous boat trip to the mainland, through a raging storm.

On a series of boats and trains to Paris they meet Irma, who also has been deserted by her lover. She is a complicated character: ageing and alcoholic, but capable of regenerating life and offering unconditional love to both Scully and Billie – a somewhat neglected Aphrodite. She intervenes at critical moments in the narrative, both frustrating and enabling their attempts to continue their journey; she also brings sexuality back into Scully's life. As he continues his journey of discovery, Billie regains her strength, and gradually transforms into Scully's parent.

Paris is the next stop on what has now become an odyssey. The family had lived there while Jennifer studied and wrote poetry, Scully working and Billie attending school. As with her painting, her poetry mentor and friends encouraged her, but in reality thought she had no talent. Jennifer contacts Scully, in order to meet. When he shows up, she runs away; he and Billie try to catch her but are unsuccessful.

The last part of their journey leads to Amsterdam, where Scully believes he has finally discovered the place to which Jennifer fled. She seems to have had an affair with a female photographer. Scully collapses, and Billie sits with him, helping him heal.

After a few days, they return to Ireland. Scully removes a rag from the wishing tree. One night, Billie discovers the riders. Scully joins her in watching. She beckons him back to their cottage; he joins her. Reality has returned.

On the symbolic level, the novel assumes a different life. The disappearance of Jennifer ruptured the Scully family. The narrative concentrates on defining the empty space between the family members who have suffered from the rupture. On this level, we see that it is liminal space, a space that will be filled with the transforming journeys of Scully, Billie and Jennifer.

Scully's pursuit of Jennifer evokes many literary parallels; it takes on some of the characteristics of Homer's *Odyssey* and, to a greater extent, Joyce's *Ulysses*. Another literary allusion is Billie's obsession with *The Hunchback of Notre Dame*.

Quasimodo is a one-eyed aberration: Scully has one good eye, Billie almost loses an eye as a result of the dog bite and Ulysses almost loses his life to the one-eyed Cyclops. Nighttown, Dublin's red-light district, in the 'Circe' episode in Joyce's *Ulysses* is similar to Scully's vision of Amsterdam. The gypsy girl in *Hunchback* reminds one of Molly Bloom as well as aspects of both Irma and Jennifer.

But, the most important shared characteristic is the journey itself:

> *The effect of the successful adventure of the hero is the unlocking and release again of the flow of life into the body of the world.*[1]

The journey is an orientation symbol; it establishes the guidelines and boundaries of explorations in liminal space on the path to individuation. Lorenz's insight into this process is germane:

> *from the point of view of Jungian depth psychology, an interior experience of ambivalence, struggle, alienation, and doubt could be the beginning of an important process, enabling an individual to overcome some of the dissociative tendencies constantly reproduced within our culture.*[2]

Even though the process being described is within the psyche, the novel's unifying motif, around which all the symbolic contents orbit is, on this level, geographic: Australia versus Europe. On the mythological level, the novel's geographic metaphor will transform into a temporal one: the old world versus the new.

The interior experience of rupture becomes the symptom that drives Scully: panic attacks regarding Jennifer's motivations and whereabouts alternate with periods of depression. These are interspersed with times of wonderful parenting. Scully's inability to understand Jennifer's disappearance is the embodiment of a natural, naïve soul. He is often described as animal-like, wild-looking, most of the time in physical disarray. He does not participate in society *per se*, but manages to earn a living doing construction work and other casual jobs. He is happy most of the time, and his naturalness and integrity place him in direct contrast to most of the European characters in the novel.

Billie is very much like Scully, physically and temperamentally. She is clearly Scully's child: he is both father and mother to her. Jennifer is, in every way, outside of the Scully–Billie dyad. She is as beautiful as Scully and Billie are unusual; she is as aloof as they are warm; she seems to have given up their love, while they seek hers. Except with a few other non-pretentious people, Scully fits in nowhere; Jennifer is exactly the opposite, forming 'friendships' with artistic dilettantes and others on the fringes of the artistic world. Scully views the marriage as a family partnership for which he will forsake much ego gratification; Jennifer seems to see the marriage as burdensome and sacrifices nothing to it while constantly attempting to nourish her own ego. Scully is loving; Jennifer is sexual. Scully is a working-class puritan, while Jennifer is an upper-class, evolving feminist. Scully is content; Jennifer is in transition. The rupture seems to have been inevitable.

Examining both sides of the ruptured relationship, we encounter a tension of opposites:

> *The repressed content must be made conscious so as to produce a tension of opposites, without which no forward movement is possible. The conscious mind is on top, the shadow underneath, . . . all consciousness perhaps without being aware of it, seeks its unconscious opposite, lacking which it is doomed to stagnation, congestion, and ossification. Life is born only of the spark of opposites.*[3]

Based upon the descriptions above, it appears that parts of Scully and Jennifer represent the shadow of the other. Sharp continues:

> *This in turn activates the process of compensation, which leads to an irrational 'third', the transcendent function.*[4]
>
> *Out of the collision of opposites the unconscious psyche always creates a third thing of an irrational nature, which the conscious mind neither expects nor understands. It presents itself in a form that is neither a straight 'yes' nor a straight 'no'.*[5]

The spark of opposites ignited the rupture. The characters' journeys, the third thing, are unconscious, and therefore symbolic. A conflict has arisen: conscious, unconscious and shadow are intra-psychic concepts, but the opposites cited in describing the relationship are inter-psychic. What is compensatory within the individuals' psyche can also be compensatory in the relationship. In the process of moving from the personal narrative to the symbolic within this novel, divergent thinking and accretion are the operative principles. Scully and Jennifer become meaningful symbols as we compare similar characteristics from the psyche of each.

We can view Scully and Jennifer individually, each with a persona. This views the rupture from the point of view of the separated parts. We can also view them as *complexio oppositorum*, 'the opposites embodied in a single image'.[6] This views the rupture from the parts themselves. A collection of psyches can be viewed as a single, contained unit. The defining characteristics of that unit can be parts or wholes of the contributing phenomena. The result, in which form is operative, becomes a symbol, which makes the relationship easier to analyse.

Winton's symbols are perfectly clear: the tension of opposites, rupture, and the journeys towards individuation are well motivated in the novel. Billie, in her evolution, assumes the position of the Divine Child, the redeeming image that leads Scully from his personally constructed chaos. The wishing tree is a magical element of transformation of the imagination. And the riders are there to project us into history. Their medievalism emphasizes the point; the journey is not geographic on the symbolic level, but temporal, into the mythological level.

The narrative brought contemporary mythology to the concept of the journey as propounded by Homer and Joyce; Joyce went so far as to chronicle Bloom's every thought using stream of consciousness. The symbolic transforms the journey into Scully's process of individuation.

We have discovered a great deal, and could continue adding detail to the observations. But we would miss an opportunity afforded by the great art of understanding of another human being.

The riders project us into the mythological/collective level. The medievalism is that part of the narrative which requires us to think symbolically; the point is not their history but the process of negotiating the path from narrative to symbol to myth: the journey *per se*.

Movement, or journeying to and from a point, implies seeking and continual modifying. The seeker is both within and outside the journey; there is self-reflection coupled with observation. In this novel, the seeker is the hidden character who motivates all of the action; that seeker is Jennifer. She is not only ruptured from Scully and Billie, but also from Australia.

The history of Australia reads like a case study from Spurr's *Rhetoric of Empire*.[7] Manning Clark's histories present a factual account of Australia's history:

> *Like the Asian, the European was attracted by the wealth of the Spice Islands, as well as by that promise of 'infinite merit' for those who converted infidels and pagans to the true religion.*[8]

> *As for the inhabitants, they were 'the miserablest people in the world', because 'setting aside their humane shape, they differ but little from brutes'.*[9]

The English government's euphemism for deporting convicts from its overcrowded and disease-ridden prisons was 'transportation'. It began in 1787, when America was no longer available, and became the Australian equivalent of original sin.

In a more impassioned chronicle, *Fatal Shore*, Hughes criticizes his countrymen: 'amnesia seemed to be a condition of patriotism'.[10]

> *An unstated bias rooted deep in Australian life seemed to wish that 'real' Australian history had begun with Australia respectability – with the flood of money from gold and wool, the opening of the continent, the creation of an Australian middle class. Behind the bright diorama of Australia Felix, lurked the convicts, some 160,000 of them, clanking their fetters in the penumbral darkness.*[11]

Lorenz points out that:

> *Depth psychology has always been a decentering dialogue between dominant cultures and silenced cultures, conscious and unconscious, self and other.*[12]

Hughes succeeded in bringing the silent culture into the Australian consciousness. Winton's novel dramatizes some of the far-reaching societal consequences emanating from Hughes' chronicle.

Eventually, Australia itself became a colonizer, re-enacting the American saga of the treatment of native populations. It became a racist, misogynous and increasingly Americanized culture from which the Scully family fled, in order to avoid its corrosive aspects, the dissociative elements constantly reproduced within the Australian culture.

Jennifer's move into liminal space followed a much greater rupture than the narrative subject of the novel. She appears only once, at the point in Paris when Scully and Billie are attempting to catch her as she runs away from them. They had agreed to meet, and she had appeared, but at the last moment she ran away after seeing them. She hid in an underground tunnel as they ran after her, feeling a profoundly moving sense of loss as they retreated into the physical, and therefore emotional, distance. Her life had completely changed.

This is the only expression we have of Jennifer's point of view; it is powerful, and different from the rest of the narrative. It is clear that Jennifer suffers as deeply as Scully and Billie, and that both she and Scully are moving towards individuation. But there is a critical difference: from his position in liminal space, Scully returns to normalization; from her position in liminal space, Jennifer seeks the redeeming image, the potential artist seeking the door to a wider spaciousness, thence to individuation. Her search for meaning, painful as it is, is divergent, leading her to the mythical realm; Scully's, painful as the circumstances are, is convergent, leading him to normality, which, in terms of the narrative, is circular – back to Ireland. Jennifer represents that component of love, for Scully and Billie, which lies beyond all others – sacrifice. In her discussion of the archetype of the victim, Cowan proposes that we look further into this archetype:

> *The person who perceives or feels him or herself as suffering for (not only from) a deity, a cause, a principle, or a beloved, experiences a different aspect of victimhood: the value of sacrifice. What redeems the suffering and anguish of the victim is not necessarily the cessation of suffering, but the experience of meaning in it.*
>
> *. . . my focus here is not on morality or virtue or selfishness, but rather on the capacity for sacrifice when the experience of victimization makes sacrifice psychologically necessary.*[13]

Jennifer is, with one brief exception, never present in the novel. And yet, her presence defines the novel. She is the unseen guide through the narrative, through the symbolic to the mythological/collective. She is Hermes guiding the seekers, but manifesting her greatest love at the very moment they found whom they were seeking.

The hero's journey is two separate channels: the hero, and the journey. The former leads us as far as a personal narrative allows; we stop at the symbolic level. The latter encourages us to continue our quest, to the mythological/collective level. It was necessary, in order to find that the seeker Scully was on the archetypal journey to individuation. His helper was Billie, and his elusive goal was Jennifer. It ended in a cabin in Ireland, where it began, watched over by forces who had been there already. Perhaps the one who sought in peace will eventually find it.

References

1 Campbell, J. *The Hero with a Thousand Faces*. New York: MFJ Books, 1949, p. 40.
2 Lorenz, H. *Depth Psychology: Meditations in the Field*. Einsiedeln: Daimon, 2000, p. 229.
3 Jung, C. *Collected Works* 7, Para. 78.
4 Sharp, D. *C. G. Lexicon*. Toronto: Inner City Books, p. 94.
5 Jung, C. *Collected Works 9, I*, Para. 285.
6 Sharp, p. 42.
7 Spurr, D. *The Rhetoric of Empire*. Durham, NC: Duke University Press, 1996.
8 Clark, M. *A Short History of Australia*. New York: Penguin, 1963, p. 15.
9 Ibid., p. 18.
10 Hughes, R. *The Fatal Shore*. New York: Vintage, 1986, p. xiv.
11 Ibid., p. xiii.
12 Lorenz, p. 239.
13 Cowen, L. *Tracking the White Rabbit: A Subversive View of Modern Culture*. East Sussex: Brunner-Routledge, 2002, pp. 88–89.

16

MAETERLINCK, IBSEN

In Chapter 12, we considered a group of painters and writers who involved themselves in some of the same issues and, particularly, the same settings during the same small period of time. In this chapter, the temporal boundaries are also narrow: 1892. Geographically, we are in Belgium, Norway and Sweden. The three plays under consideration are Maeterlinck's *Pelléas and Mélisande*,[1] and Ibsen's *The Master Builder*.[2] These two plays were written during a period of important changes in writing for the theatre. In discussing these two, it is necessary to accept their context. It is essential that the time period of creation and first performances is taken into account.

Freud was becoming one of the most important critical thinkers in history; his *Interpretation of Dreams* was first published in 1899 and his 'talking cure' was gaining acceptance as a means of treating mental illness. This had been preceded by the nineteenth century's understanding of the unconscious. Freud was eventually as meaningful to social and cultural history as Darwin. In addition, Marxism was beginning to penetrate social (as well as economic) theory; Einstein's physics and mathematics were challenging the earlier visions of the universe; Wagner had already permanently altered the language of music; communication and industrialization had changed the inner and outer landscapes.

Into this cultural mix, the two distinctly different plays, listed above, emerged. Unlike the similarities of various plays immediately preceding these three and the cultural acceleration of which they were a part, these scripts were not like each other. In point of fact, they were each quite different from each other, and from the general output of their time. In fact, all of the arts were undergoing this transition; for example, the music of Mahler, Scriabin, Rachmaninoff, Strauss, Stravinsky and Schoenberg was created and existed simultaneously.

In the world of playwriting, dramatic action through dialogue enabled each character in a play to present their position – a story when something in particular happened. Whereas *Pelléas and Mélisande* is part myth and part fairy tale, *Miss Julie* is a psychological drama while *The Master Builder* is more of a drama in social realism.

Pelléas and Mélisande is partially a fairy tale wrapped around a myth, as well as a myth wrapped around a fairy tale when focused upon the main characters; it is also a study in dramatic characterizations, psychologically driven in the play as an entirety. Unlike the tragic conclusion of *Melancholia*, where the tragic conclusion from the opera *Tristan and Isolde* is missing, the death of Mélisande is not a dramatic moment in the play. *The Master Builder* is a study in psychological realities of the day.

★

Maeterlinck forces certain questions: what is reality? What are symbols? What governs the choice of one or the other? How can one mix the two, successfully?

Pelléas and Mélisande is the focus of attention in this chapter, and continues as such in the next when it becomes the source of four musical works; they were composed soon after its appearance on the dramatic stage. Two of these works were influential in music that succeeded them; there is a ballet, orchestral suite, tone poem and opera.

In Maeterlinck's play, with its multi-faceted structure, it is difficult to know where reality is to be found. What is actually occurring? This is somewhat equivalent to the confusion sometimes experienced in determining the difference between background and foreground.

More concentration and energy are required of the audience in decoding what is striving towards X in an artefact such as *Pelléas and Mélisande*, compared to *The Master Builder*. The latter two offer great theatre with the insight gained from their dialogues. Their words work towards understanding, from a recognition of particular societal and psychological issues. It is probably true that Ibsen's clarity had a greater appeal for the audiences of the day, compared with Strindberg; Maeterlinck was probably referred to as an experience.

While reading some biographical studies of Maeterlinck, I continually encountered the word 'symbol'. I believe that 'symbol' is a way of observing a world devolving into the unreality of fairy tales and myths, as a means of attaining greater understanding of the unconscious – and then, returning to the deepest reality. Schorske writes that 'symbolism' was 'born out of disintegrating naturalism'.[4] (I must admit to a discomfort in the use of the 'ism' type of definition or, for that matter, with most examples of jargon.) When I use the term, or derivative of 'symbol', I simply refer to a substitution of one word or object for another, designed to engage curiosity or to supply a certain type of knowledge.

Pelléas and Mélisande is part fairy tale, based upon Rapunzel, and part retelling of the Tristan myth; the latter is presented in everyday dialogue with complete, intelligible sentences. It is realistic and is constantly moving the story forward.

It is an archetypal tragic love story. Maeterlinck decorates the story with insertions of fairy tale utterances; the basic overall structure is therefore somewhat obscured. Although our mode of predictive thinking attempts to put us into the mode in which the love story-myth unfolds, the alternation with the unreality of the fairy tale sections keeps the audience off balance. Sophistication on the part of the audience is offset by a lack of clarification – there is no constant flow of drama.

In one sense, Maeterlinck is mimicking some of the aspects of Impressionist painters and composers; images are confined in blurred boundaries. Mélisande speaks in short, exclamatory phrases without syntax – brief, constantly repetitive phrases. This is more pronounced at the beginning and ending of the play, but a feeling of Mélisande's dissociation permeates the entire play. We know something is there, inside of her psyche; we do not have to re-order reality – as in Cubism. We are in a state of simultaneously knowing and not knowing. Mélisande's passivity is inescapable. Her depression is reminiscent of the melancholia displayed by Justine in *Melancholia*. It is the dramatization of Mélisande's unconscious; to her consciousness, it seems that reality cannot be accessed.

When Mélisande first appears, she encounters Golaud. They are in the forest, by a spring – both manifestations of the unconscious. Golaud quizzes her, but she is traumatized, unable to converse or communicate. The physical says much – but we don't know what it means. At this point in the drama, it could be an eerie, threatening place.

As in a well-conceived piece of music, our expectations are in motion from the beginning of the work. In the music – in the forest with Mélisande and Golaud – we are aware of something not being right, and we, as an audience ever-seeking the X that the creator wants to give us . . . sit and wait. (Expectation and either its frustration or fulfilment are a critical feature of all time-bound creations.)

The passivity of Mélisande, in contrast to the aggressiveness of Golaud, creates a tension of opposites, from which their baby, prematurely born just prior to Mélisande's death, could possibly be considered a production of a third – a reconciliation.

At the end of the play, Mélisande dies from a wound given her by Golaud just after killing Pelléas. This powerful event brought her back to her initial traumatic mood. The baby to whom she gave premature birth was born 'sickly'.

Throughout the play, there are various references to the kingdom in peril; the prevailing consciousness is in turmoil. The reality of the failing social structure, and the fantasy life of the mysterious, vapour-like being of Mélisande, are the places where the fantasy of the fairy tale and the reality of the myth directly clash – in conjunction with the decaying society. The baby represents the new generation . . . ill from the start.

The danger to this society, both old and new, is Golaud. Every character seems aware of his ambition to rule. But like so many issues articulated in the play, no one can do anything about it. Golaud eventually runs amok after interpreting a conversation with Yniold that seemed to verify that Pelléas and Mélisande were lovers. The lives of his half-brother and his wife are sacrificed on the fantasy of his young child.

Maeterlinck has still not provided answers to the questions asked earlier. What if the script does not make sense? Or, should we be trying to make sense of it? It is relatively easy to pick out mosaics here and there, but eventually they must begin to form a meaningful entirety.

This is one of the main elements of the new music of the time, in particular Debussy. It is no accident that Pelléas and Mélisande was the text that Debussy chose for his opera, of the same name, and of exactly the same text.

Pieces of mosaic do not necessarily point to conclusions, but they do allow for continuing the process of seeking answers.

The author gives us several opportunities to realize that the kingdom, which Golaud will inherit from his father, Arkel, is slowly dying. In the beginning, we find Mélisande fearful of Golaud; both are lost. Soon – although time frames are impossible to calculate – Mélisande and Golaud are married . . . about which Golaud's parents, Arkel and Geneviève, are suspicious. They feel they have been deceived without having their eyes open. These parents dwell in reality, the recently married couple in fantasy.

In spite of the inability of anyone to articulate the existence of these alternate universes, they continue to exist in this symbiotic fashion. Golaud causes grief in both of them. Golaud is fearful of Arkel's disapproval (pp. 26–27), a projection of his unwise, tempestuous nature. Maeterlinck has created a reality versus fantasy scenario; as the reality that is the kingdom falls apart, fantasy is the means by which he can achieve the continuity of his play; there are still many mosaics waiting to be added. One way of doing this is seen in the remarkable section (Act 3, Scene 3) in one of the towers of the castle. Pelléas and Mélisande are having a conversation that approaches intimacy when her hair comes loose and spills out all around her. Pelléas is enthralled by it – he playfully suggests binding her to the branches of a tree outside.

The action in *Rapunzel* begins with a Faustian bargain: the new baby in trade for some vegetables from the garden of the enchantress. We have already experienced this archetype in *The Fisherman and His Wife*, in the chapter dealing with *To the Lighthouse*. The type of Faustian bargain in Maeterlinck's play was essentially the reason for Mélisande's marriage to Golaud. One of her greatest fears was that of being abandoned, as she had been by her mother. Yniold had the same fear; his mother (Golaud's first wife) died while he was very young, which he experienced as abandonment. Mélisande says to Pelléas near the end of the play: 'Why do you always tell me that you must go away?' (Act 4, Scene 4).

Bettelheim writes: 'There is no greater threat in life than that we will be deserted, left all alone.' In supporting the actions of the enchantress over those of Rapunzel's parents who made the Faustian bargain, Bettelheim offers this: 'To love so selfishly and foolishly is wrong, but not evil.'[5]

Golaud was evil in his total lack of self-control. Pelléas and Mélisande were living in the fantasy world; their timidity in connecting with each other kept them in their world of unreality, unable to show that they had the last mosaic.

★

We move from the incomplete mosaic fantasy to the natural life setting of *The Master Builder*. Maeterlinck, through his alternations of fairy tales with mythic dramas, left the play suspended; characters did die, but many existential questions remained. Neither Mélisande's background nor motivations were ever clear. The simplicity of the story contrasted with the complexity of its unfolding. Usually, this would suggest that an archetype was, after a thorough reduction, about to appear. But the motivation for the lovers' actions was deliberately obscured. An unmotivated and oddly discontinuous narrative presents little motivation for audience involvement.

Two possibilities present themselves for attaining further clarification of this type of play: an in-depth psychoanalytical study of Pelléas, Mélisande and Golaud; or, perhaps, an opera based upon the text. As we shall see in the next chapter, music in the form of opera became a solution. In the next chapter, we will focus on Debussy's opera *Pelléas and Mélisande*, as well as three other pieces – branches from Maeterlinck's tree.

The next two plays have none of the theatrical issues present in the Maeterlinck play. In the study of Ibsen's *The Master Builder*, we find different types of dramaturgical issue. In its study of the Solness family and the characters associated with the life-changing moment in their lives, life is as it is lived. Not that all is well, for it is not. But unlike the Maeterlinck play, the kingdom of 1892 Norway is flourishing. There is no sign of the universal catastrophe we encountered in *Pelléas and Mélisande* or *Melancholia*.

In Ibsen's play, insecurities and deceits are interwoven into the play's fabric. Sadness rules nearly all of the characters, with the exception of Doctor Herdahl who is the scientific, logical realist in the group. He, together with Mrs Solness, is sceptical about Hilde Wangel throughout the play. Among the main characters, there are uncertainties in almost every utterance. It is not that there is a lack of reality, but rather a lack of believability. Some of the events chronicled by the main characters actually did occur; many of them, especially spoken by Hilde, conceivably did not.

After the aesthetic uncertainties that confronted the audience in *Pelléas and Mélisande*, questions surrounding the subject of reality are still present. In Maeterlinck, reality is a by-product of the efforts of the audience in putting together small bits of information into a framework of meaning. Linear time is without presence; various scenes occur without being part of a notable timeline.

In *The Master Builder*, reality is determined by the actions and dialogue of the characters, even if the boundaries shift as various fantasies/delusions appear, and reappear. The timeline is continuous, although memory does play a significant role.

The dialogues and actions of the play focus upon three characters: Solness, age 63-plus, the master builder, mean spirited to most others, professionally successful, wounded to the point of paranoia, naïve in the presence of young women; Mrs Solness, his wife, utterly devoid of hope, without resilience or the ego strength necessary to function in the patriarchy of 1890s Norway; Hilde Wangel, age 23, a predator, delusional, governed by fantasies, who enters from Solness' past – perhaps.

Hilde arrived at the Solness home unannounced, unexpected and uninvited. She completes a triangular structure that strongly links the main characters to each other through a group of complexes that, because of the various levels of ego-investment or absence of ego, can become unlinked at any angle where two lines meet. The dramatic problem for the audience is to understand the nature of the complexes that form the binding lines. (This is the territory of the depth psychologist, which is why I suggested that these three plays be considered from that perspective. This differs from the usual relationship that exists between analyst and analysand for the simple reason that the entire case is presented in completed format, whereas the case would normally function over time.) Answers appear late in the play, and are hardly audible/visible. But they do occur in linear time; Ibsen wants his realities to be known, and accessible.

The first scene introduces several of the play's conflicts; it occurs in the Solness house and involves a satellite issue of the Broviks – father and son – and Kaya, fiancée of Ragnar, the younger Brovik. The elder Brovik is an integral worker in the office of Solness; originally, Solness worked for Brovik, but managed to wrest control from him and is now the boss in the home-building firm. Ragnar is an ambitious young architect, being held back by Solness' fears and jealousy of youth. The paranoia surrounding the idea of youth is complicated by the relationships they both have with Kaya – another triangle.

It is unclear why Solness wants to keep Kaya in his office, except that she is extremely useful to him. Meanwhile, Kaya has formed a close attachment to Solness, which is both personal and professional. The need among the three is important, but plays a secondary role in what follows. Kaya had silently thought that Solness and she had reached some sort of 'agreement' about their future together. Throughout the play, words are misinterpreted to the detriment of the listener.

Mrs Solness appears and voices her sarcasm regarding Solness' alleged need for keeping Kaya in his employ. The sarcastic jealousy that Mrs Solness displays intensifies as Hilde begins solidifying her attempts to control Solness. However, Mrs Solness is never fooled by her husband's childish interest in younger women; her jealousy is well-founded.

With Hilde's arrival, we are also introduced to Solness' paranoid fear of youth taking over, and putting him out of business, and life. This is manifested in his ill-treatment of Ragnar. But paranoia encompasses more: namely, some sort of attachment from the outside.

In this expository scene, Solness also remarks to the doctor about his concern for Mrs Solness and the guilt he feels regarding the 'debt' he owes her. He adds that he has been lucky all his life. In these brief words, Solness has opened the central part of his historical narrative, which is the burning down of their previous home, 13 years ago, and the consequent deaths of their infant sons.

Here is a complete narrative, with inclusions from later in the play that modified the situation. It was winter. A chimney caught fire and the house burned to the ground. Mrs Solness and the babies escaped; soon thereafter, the babies died. Possibly, it was the ice cold weather to which they were exposed. It later became clear that Mrs Solness was the one who became very ill from the exposure; her milk became infected, and it killed the babies.

As the story unfolds throughout the play, it is revealed that the fire actually began in a different room. It was not the carelessly forgotten leak in the chimney, for which Solness blamed himself; he knew about it but did not fix it. Nonetheless, Solness persisted in feeling responsible; Mrs Solness felt it was the work of God.

Solness felt that the burned house allowed him to begin to flourish as a builder of homes because his business grew. His fear of youth, perhaps a manifestation of his guilt over the death of his twins, and its appearance could make his luck change for the worse. New design ideas, building concepts and ways of dealing with potential clients were emerging. Solness must have seen these developments in Ragnar, particularly in the group of drawings he left for Solness' criticism. As he expressed this theory to the doctor – youth would come 'banging on the door . . . saying make way!' – there was a banging on the door. It was the entrance of Hilde.

I must admit that I do not understand the crudeness of this gesture – unless Ibsen was merely having fun with his audience. Hilde's presence in the story brings an entirely new dimension to it – that of fantasy delusion. While the narrative of the Solness family, painful as it is, conforms to reality insofar as facts are concerned, with Hilde we must ask about the veracity of her reminiscences of Solness some ten years earlier.

There are two different approaches to Hilde's claim of previous association with Solness: they are either the fantasies of a delusional mind or they are a series of correctly remembered events. I have chosen the former, because at no time – except for one brief moment of semi-agreement near the play's conclusion – does Solness really accept Hilde's depiction of their previous 'relationship'. On the other hand, she presents herself as having a disturbed childhood; she left home at 13 and never returned, and had she returned she would have been 'caged up'. She is quite mature in the sexual manipulation of Solness; and, her own sexual cravings are quite evident. Simultaneously, she is an anti-patriarchal free spirit.

But the most pronounced issue leading me to think that her presentations are fantasies is her constant repetition of her desire for a 'castle in the air', of which she would be the 'princess'. This is ultimately a fairy tale projection, displaying a need for safety. As a result of her insistent passive-aggressive thrusts, Solness gradually came to believe her delusions of the future; this could have partly been a by-product of his sexual attraction to Hilde. Remember that she could also offer the possibility of bearing children for him, children for his new house, and possible compensation for his feelings of guilt.

The third line of this catastrophe-in-waiting is Mrs Solness. She is openly mistrustful of Solness' attention to Kaya and Hilde. She is truly 'caged up' in the gloom of the Solness household, although much of it clearly emanates from her. Her constant claim of doing her 'duty' is bothersome. Repetition of a complaint – her anti-patriarchal sarcasm – is her only opportunity to express her feelings regarding her circumstance as the household's female functionary. But the one thing that she can use to wound Solness and gather emotional response from others is the tragic death of her babies. She is consumed with guilt and has totally lost her feeling function; she is without emotion, and displays no affect. This behaviour defends her from a psychotic break; there can be no boiling over if there is no stove. She is surprised when Solness confesses his feelings of guilt about the fire, and speaks of owing a debt to her. He claims that he cannot speak to her about his feelings – she is 'waste', 'barren'. This is an admission on Solness' part of the pain and despair he feels about the absence of the children, but no overt effort to do something about it seemed to occur to either of them. For Solness, compensation could have been achieved through sexual relationships with either Kaya or Hilde. But Mrs Solness avoids a meaningful conversation; the fire, and deaths, were God's will.

The second triangle (Solness, Kaya and Ragnar) is broken as a result of Hilde's anger at Solness' treatment of Ragnar. Solness belittles Ragnar's drawings, fully aware of their value, but caught in the paranoid fear of youth. Hilde criticizes his harsh treatment of Ragnar, demanding that he write complimentary critiques on the drawings for Ragnar's dying father to see; his father had already died. A confrontation follows, where Kaya realizes that Solness no longer has any need of her. Solness fires Ragnar and Kaya, and they are released to lead their own lives – no longer caged.

The path to individuation, of a sort, has run from the elder Brovik through Solness to Ragnar. It is 'only' because Solness is neither an architect (he never finished his training) nor a master builder; it is a title he gave himself. Grandiosity is enlisted to reinforce the paranoid fear of youth taking over. In firing Ragnar, Solness provided him with the encouragement to actually be that very youth. To all else that disturbs Solness, we must consider self-destructiveness; reality bears this out.

*

The final, and most important, actual event occurs at the end of the play. Solness' new house has been completed, and tradition requires that a wreath be placed at its highest point. Hilde had first experienced Solness as he was climbing to the top of the spire of a recently completed church in Lysanger; he sang some sort of song, and after laying the wreath returned to the ground. Since then, he has developed an intense fear of heights, and despite Hilde's coaxing is 'not so sure' he wants to climb to the top. Everyone attempts to dissuade him – except Hilde.

The conclusion of the play recaps the various complexes that have governed the behaviours of Solness and Hilde. Hilde uses her complete repertoire of persuasions on Solness, enticing him with assurances that conquering the height would be beneficial to his sexual prowess – citing the Vikings in her manipulations. (They appeared earlier as an apparition of Hilde's sexuality.) She linked the presence on top of the house with her desire for a castle in the air – she told him that he owed it to her. He responded by inquiring whether it was safe to hide in castles in the air.

The path to completing our understanding ends close to the play's conclusion. Solness explains to Hilde that he is afraid, not of death, but of retribution. God-guilt is more powerful than death. He had pious parents and felt it was his 'duty' to build churches. He, too, was imprinted with the religious concept of duty. However, he managed to cut loose from the trolls and demons about whom both he and Hilde had spoken, several times. They were cited to validate his luck, and her fantasies.

This led to the fire, God's vengeance. At Lysander, Solness declared his freedom. He felt that he had lived a pious life, and thought that 'He' should be pleased with him. Hilda questions to which 'He' he is referring – an enormously cutting question/remark.

The question from Hilde is the end of this thread. Is Solness afraid of God or of his pious father? His father complex emerges as subtly as did Hilde's 'caged up' feeling. The aggression of her complex attacks the weaknesses of his; he climbs to the top of the spire, sings a song to God and falls to his death.

★

Ibsen and Maeterlinck wrote their plays in the same year. Maeterlinck created a love story using fantasy as the binding element; Ibsen created a story of natural life settings with natural life characters. We are speaking of the natural life of 1892, and, although the psychological complexities are articulated in contemporary terms, the characters' behaviours must be accepted in their historical contexts. We may feel a bit uncomfortable with the words and actions of the characters, but emotional connections – the case histories to which I referred – are present in countless consultation rooms every day.

References

1 Maeterlinck, M. *Pelléas and Mélisande*. Amsterdam: Fredonia Books, 2001.
2 Ibsen, H. *Plays: One*. London: Methuen Drama World Classics, 1980.

17
PELLÉAS AND MÉLISANDE

The subtitle for Part Two is 'The end of boundaries'. In this last chapter, I want to explore how the transition away from symbolic theatre was immediately followed by the conclusion of eighteenth–nineteenth-century musical thinking, including tonality; both were ways of breaking through boundaries that allowed for a veritable flood of new techniques for musical composition.

Coupled with the mystery of Maeterlinck's drama, the cultural world was about to be altered. Romanticism was mostly gone; this lasted until the mid-twentieth century, until Mahler was resurrected as adventurous conductors joined those in Amsterdam who had continuously promoted his music. A central question to be asked is how and why this particular play had so much influence on the future of music? Was it, in fact, the play itself? If so, was it because of what was said . . . or was it because of what was left unsaid . . . or was it because of the way it was said?

Within a few years after the play's introduction, four composers wrote pieces based upon *Pelléas and Mélisande*: Fauré (1898) wrote incidental music for the play; Sibelius (1906) wrote music for the ballet; Schoenberg (1903) wrote a tone poem; and Debussy wrote an opera (1902). I will not focus on either Fauré or Sibelius, since their works did not make the same historical contributions as those of Schoenberg and Debussy. Both Fauré and Sibelius excerpted suites (collections of movements) from their works, and both named their movements so as to vaguely keep them attached to the play. But neither has been particularly important in the concert repertoire.

The compositions of both Debussy and Schoenberg changed the sound of music; they influenced a significant group of composers – definitely not all, however. Basic to our understanding of the language of music, and how these changes represented not only a cultural shift but also a deeply probing aspect of the unconscious as it attempts to come to grips with these new phenomena, it would be an incomplete understanding without realizing that these conditions of aesthetic change affected all of the arts – and therefore the entire psyche. Melody, harmony and orchestration all began to change in the first decade of the twentieth century; Debussy and Schoenberg were the leaders of these changes.

Wagner had permanently altered the trajectory of that musical language called 'tonality', but other dramatic changes had occurred before his time. Music of the Renaissance epoch was mostly a period of religious functions though there was a healthy presence of popular/folk songs and dances. This epoch had been preceded by the medieval epoch, in which much of the music was based on, if not directly using, Gregorian chant; the religious music had a narrow melodic verbal flow that allowed for phrasings that made most of the text intelligible.

The solemnity of the religious music and the increasing popularity of folk and dance music heralded a new world mind-set in Western Europe. Secular music, singing and musical instruments all appeared. At the end of this epoch, we encounter the music of two of the greatest composers: Josquin des Prez and Claudio Monteverdi.

During the next epoch, the Baroque, harmonies became more colourful as separate voices coalesced into vertical groupings. Music governed by the movement of individual voices (counterpoint) became music governed by groupings related to a bass note (harmony). The music of Bach was the high point of this epoch. If we add to this Beethoven, Wagner and the two composers we are discussing, we find that the greatest composers of the era occur near its conclusion, and that endings of old ideas and styles become beginnings of new ideas. It was in the midst of the actual epochs that musical concepts were being formulated. During the Classic epoch, which reached its apex with Beethoven, Haydn and Mozart were codifying musical forms, based upon certain harmonic practices, with melodies derived from the harmony. It was this model that Wagner broke, and until Schoenberg the harmony of Tristan model was the rule. In point of fact, the entire period 1650–1900 was the 'common practice' period, which includes both a journey to and from the music of Wagner. In order to understand this more profoundly, we must transfer our point of entry into Debussy and Schoenberg to linguistics.

★

Basic to our understanding of music is that it is a language. The premise of linguistics rests upon semantics and syntax. Semantics is what words mean; syntax is how they are used. Most, if not all, languages have words that mean more than one thing; in that case, it is almost always the situation that context will clarify meaning. Another important aspect of language is how it sounds – phonology. Every language has a unique melody; one can imitate a language by this alone. In doubt? Please refer to Danny Kaye in the film *The Inspector General* or the Swedish Chef in *The Muppet Show*.

In addition to the melody of the language, emphasis is important. The classic linguistic example is the sentence 'I like her cooking'. Repeating the sentence four times while, in turn, accenting a different word, yields four different meanings.

The context shifts the meaning using emphasis only, while semantics and syntax remain the same. Of the many methods for analysing language, phonologically is the most interesting for musicians. But the combination of the three aspects listed, combined with information theory and the gestalt psychology of Leonard Meyer, plus the logical processes of Susanne Langer, have allowed persons studying the art of music to converse authoritatively, in place of using jargon.

In the early years of the twentieth century, Debussy and Schoenberg were about to create new worlds of music, replacing that of common practice. Debussy inherited the French rationality of what would become the philosophical and literary concepts of existentialism, and the painters' vision that was Impressionism. Semantically, he used triads from his European predecessors, but because they were used in a different syntax, their context changed them quite a bit. In the tone poem that we are discussing, Schoenberg also used the same syntax, but the texture is so cluttered that it is hard to recognize them; since syntax relies on clarity of semantics, Schoenberg sounds totally different from Debussy.

Schoenberg inherited the world of expression of Munch and Ernst, of Freud and of Mahler. His romantic vocabulary was an extension of Wagner's, and the resultant power of non-harmonic tones described earlier. Schoenberg is chromatic while Debussy is modal – meaning their basic structures evolved from different types of scale. The best way to get these ideas in your own ears is to listen to both of these pieces. Your ears will act as the pathway to what you want to know – to knowledge.

During his compositional life, especially beginning around 1918, Schoenberg developed an entirely new musical language: the 12-tone technique. It is important to note that in his earlier music, which includes *Pelléas and Mélisande*, he was composing music similar in semantics and syntax, but not phonology, to that of Mahler and Strauss. But that all changed with the onset of the 12-tone idea. Instead of scales or modes of seven tones each, he replaced them with a series of the 12 notes within an octave, all of which had to be used before any could be repeated. It substituted these series for tonality, in a counter-intuitive process that had a fairly short lifespan. But he was also an astute purveyor of his concept, and managed to respond to his critics by shaming them. His serial technique became more attractive as time progressed. Music of this genre serialized all aspects of music; there was nothing that was not precompositionally ordered. This process of total serialization led to computer use in music, and thereafter computer-generated electronic music. At this point (1970 or thereabout) two reactions set in: minimalism and New Romanticism.

During his early atonal, but not yet his 12-tone, works, Schoenberg constructed new concepts for an audience; it could find no emotion in the music, music that seemed to have lost its power to project feeling. His great success, then, was to provide art, perhaps for the first time, with a reason to avoid it. It is, however, important to bear in mind that total serialism and the complexities that went with it were basically relegated to academic audiences; do not misunderstand me . . . there is nothing inherently wrong with this artistic segregation, or that the academic world formed a somewhat discrete part of it. But it does pose the question: what is music, or any art, without an X?

Boundaries, in the arts, do not really exist. What the metaphor addresses is that point in cultural accumulation, in all creative media, where saturation becomes obvious. Both Debussy and Schoenberg were simultaneously at that point – the over-bloating of Romanticism in music. It is critical to note that certain composers were active during boundary-evoking periods – 'boundary-evoking' in the sense that a shift became necessary in the musical culture – and there was a significant composer present to initiate it. Thus, there were Josquin des Prez and Monteverdi, Bach, Beethoven, Wagner and Mahler – all composers who both closed an era and opened a new one. We can finalize the recognition of metaphor in the period under discussion (1890s–1910s) by examining the text setting and orchestration techniques of the two composers.

Schoenberg's treatment of the Maeterlinck play is that of a tone poem: an orchestral work without text that musically illustrates a story. Schoenberg did attempt to follow the outlines of the story, with more success than Fauré or Sibelius; this gave a certain continuity to the work. It is noteworthy that, in the twentieth century, the tone poem evolved into the one-movement symphony form. Both attempted to tell a story, but the symphony's was textless; there was no attachment to a text, but often the sheer power of the music tells its own, purely musical, story.

Translating the symbols in the text into musical symbols is highly personal; it is a symbol of a symbol. Schoenberg had to be content with a personal statement about how he perceived and felt about the text . . . in music. He does have sections and thematic material in which he singles out Mélisande, Pelléas and Golaud, in certain scenes from the play.

Schoenberg orchestrated in orchestral families; that is, confining the textures to like-sounding instruments. He seldom left open musical space to allow for colour clarity or for crossing of orchestral groupings that mark Debussy's technique. Schoenberg's main source of emotional flexibility was in changes of tempo and in his use of dynamics, either by addition or subtraction of volume.

Debussy began the era of the New Romanticism by changes in the use of colour. (Romanticism had never vanished. It survived within the context of nationalist composers. When it returned in the 1970s, it was a powerful reminder that there are beautiful qualities in music.) But at the time, the music of Debussy and Schoenberg was the music of the Western world, music of the developing *avant garde*, on the verge of openings in the rest of the world that would add to the continuing changes in the medium of music.

The discussion of Maeterlinck, and the comparisons with Ibsen and Strindberg, were a lengthy introduction to Debussy's opera *Pelléas and Mélisande*. Other authors of plays and operas were available; what attracted Debussy to Maeterlinck? I would suggest that it was the challenge of non-certainty – an extension of the Jungian concept of acausal reality – usually referred to as 'synchronicity'. There is a mystery to be solved in the Maeterlinck text . . . as there is in Debussy's setting; text and music were a perfect match.

Debussy's music is of critical importance to the manner in which music developed in the twentieth century; it shifted the fundamental gesture of music to colour. It is far removed from the precompositional numbers of Schoenberg. For Debussy, the orchestra canvas was to be painted upon with all the instrumental colour resources available. His orchestration included a wide variety of chamber ensembles. The thinned backdrop of orchestral colour guarantees that the leitmotifs will be heard.

Debussy used his intuition regarding the power of colour to create a new musical universe. He left spaces in the orchestra texture where no instrument is sounding, leaving room for the overtones to do their job of enforcing the colours. It is equivalent to phonology in music. Listening to his opera, one becomes aware of a different quality to the vocal parts. Debussy projects a text that is something that catches much of the melody of the French language. The voice is clearly heard and, hopefully, understood. This removes that quality of opera which yields all control to the singers, the orchestra being there for background and comment. In Wagner, the voice had become another instrument, fully integrated into the orchestra – as an equal, not a superior. Debussy's opera opened a new avenue of drama: a type of spoken opera.

To return to something previously suggested: it may have been some kind of mysterious challenge that attracted Debussy to Maeterlinck. Lack of certainty was part of the turn of the twentieth century's bequest to the twenty-first. Statements of certainty in one culture contrasted with suggestions of possibility in another. Semantics (chord formations) remained the same until the Schoenbergian 12-tone epoch began the second decade of the new century. Syntactically, both pieces were denied the expectation/fulfilment process inherent in tonality. Visions in all of the arts opened up new pathways into the unconscious, in creators and audiences. It is a small step to begin this journey of understanding.

★

Unlike the other creator discussed in these pages, Debussy and Schoenberg stood at the threshold of an epoch – the music of the twentieth century. They led, they were followed; they did not complete the steps that others would take. They completed great works of art, penetrating the unconscious with a group of new openings, through which others would be guided: Dutilleux and Messiaen, Berg and Dallapiccola . . . others realized what Debussy and Schoenberg had done.

But in a different milieu, composers maintained a reinvigorated sense of tonality, mainly from a perspective of semantics, but a variety of personal syntaxes emerged that spoke to many throughout the world. Those who were deeply moved by Mahler remained: in the depth of Britten, the mysticism of Tavener, the direct connection with Albert and Schwantner, the sheer brilliance of Adams and the immense power of Schuman . . . as well as many others. Standing at the gateway to the twentieth century's meeting with its unconscious psyche, two composers reached out and showed us a pathway.

18

FINALE

Why I wrote this book

Unfolding the Unconscious Psyche is about how we understand the arts. I began with the idea of starting a conversation based upon asking questions of works of art in various media: that is, by asking the works themselves. A few words on how this came about, and the people who aided me on the personal journey.

It began simply enough. A brilliant teacher opened a graduate seminar that I was attending with the following question: 'Why is the *Musical Joke* funny?' In the intervening decades, I have posed this same question to my graduate students: at the first class, and then again at the last class. The first time: there is close to absolute silence, a few snickers, uneasy stirrings in seats, probably even some prayers that somebody – anybody – would answer the question. The second time: they wouldn't stop talking. I had to squeeze in a nostalgic farewell, departing a roomful of squabbling future professors, who undoubtedly would someday ask the same questions of their students.

1. *Why even ask the question?*
2. *What does it mean?*
3. *What, above all, is the answer?*
4. *Do all Californians ask such stupid questions?*

1. Because it is interesting to think about.
2. It means you now have permission to think completely outside the boundaries within which your previous education has imprisoned you.
3. Study Leonard B. Meyer first. Then, again. Repeat until you know the answer.
4. Yes, I certainly hope so.

I owe my intellectual life to pursuing that type of question, as I assume readers of this book have already figured out. The reason I have pursued these questions is because they matter.

*

Thank yous traditionally precede the text. I prefer this closing chapter for them, hoping that the beacons of light they constantly offered me are observable to the reader.

My teachers: Robert Tusler, in all music, from the Renaissance to the day of the tutorial; nothing was left without discussion. When we were through with a certain topic, we would do it all over again . . . changing the musical examples. We spent a phenomenal amount of time together; his office was always filled with excitement. Henri Lazarof: my composition teacher, who made me accountable for every note on the page. He was rough, sometimes gruff, and the most wonderful teacher any future composer could have had.

There are others, who introduced me to the work of Jung, and were always available for leading me to understanding of his work. Deanne Newman: Jungian analyst, friend of so many years, helped me with kindness, tolerated my arguments with her about what I had just read but with which she had lived for decades – forever patient, understanding and humorous. Lyn Cowan: Jungian analyst and scholar, whose powerful books helped me understand how to write with words (notes and symphonies are so much easier), who had a way of untangling some ill-formed ideas and found what I was really talking about, a sounding board who read my manuscript and encouraged me to continue. And Jim Hollis: Jungian analyst and scholar, who guided me to the opening of the first door that was to become this book, by simply pointing out that it was there. I relish the moment when I can gratefully put the printed copy of this book in his hands.

And finally, my wife, Beth. The unconscious psyche is an important part of all of us. It is a life-asserting presence, and to access it is to accept challenges of which we're only minutely aware. The unconscious has ways of protecting itself – the ego – in order to be able to live a completely placid life. Encountering that unknown, but not unknowable, part of oneself is difficult, even threatening. This is why I felt it necessary to show how first we can encounter the unconscious through the manner in which others have done it.

This life-asserting presence, of which I have repeatedly spoken as romanticism, in the past was something I was often tempted to avoid; but it was always sought after. Not always successful, it was Beth's readings, comments and discussions, and nearly undecipherable notes that kept me on track. It takes courage, trust and love to tell someone that he's missing his own point – with a smile and a hug. In this atmosphere, I allowed myself to unfold the unconscious psyche.

INDEX